TOILET TRAINING— THE EASY WAY!

Toilet training your child can be easier than you ever expected. Now, with this clear, concise guide, you can say good-bye to diapers—and find out . . .

- **How your attitude can make training go more quickly and smoothly**
- **How to handle setbacks**
- **Which techniques are the most effective for your child**
- **How to decide when the time is right**
- **How to instill discipline with love**
- **How to meet the needs of children in special situations**

and more

GOOD-BYE DIAPERS

GOOD-BYE DIAPERS

Batya Swift Yasgur

Produced by The Philip Lief Group, Inc.

BERKLEY BOOKS, NEW YORK

GOOD-BYE DIAPERS

A Berkley Book / published by arrangement with
The Philip Lief Group, Inc.

PRINTING HISTORY
Berkley edition / April 1994

ISBN: 0–425–14185–3

BERKLEY®
Berkley Books are published by The Berkley Publishing Group,
200 Madison Avenue, New York, New York 10016.
BERKLEY and the "B" design
are trademarks belonging to Berkley Publishing Corporation.

PRINTED IN THE UNITED STATES OF AMERICA

10 9 8 7 6

952086

Dedicated to the memory of Jeremiah . . .
the echo in my heart

ACKNOWLEDGMENTS

It is a pleasure to write acknowledgments, because doing so gives me the opportunity to thank many wonderful people:

First and foremost, it is hard to know how to express in words the gratitude and love I feel toward Barry (''Bears'') and Suzi Kaufman, founders and directors of the Option Institute and Fellowship in Sheffield, Massachusetts. I can't imagine what my life would be like today if I hadn't read their books, listened to their tapes, and been gifted with the rich, varied experiences of dialogues, programs, training, and personal discussions with them. My parenting has been forever transformed in a wondrous, miraculous way as a result of the Kaufmans' input. This book, too, would not have been possible without their profound impact on my thinking. Thank you so much.

Many thanks as well to my other friends and mentors at the Option Institute: Gary Skow, Steven and Gita Wertz, Ron Bjarnason, Bonnie Pfeiffer, Ann Bianchi, Mecki Augustein, and Susan Abrams in particular come to mind. Thanks, too, to my many other Option friends who walk a common path toward love and happiness with me, including Kathleen Sullivan, Peter Borelli, and Carmela Rotter.

Although I'm not personally acquainted with either of them, I'd like to express my appreciation to Dr. Bernie

Siegel, author of such seminal works as *Love Medicine and Miracles* and to Dr. Gerold Jampolsky, author of *Love Is Letting Go of Fear*, among other major books, for their contribution to my life and thought. Their writings have exercised a profound impact on my own parenting, my relationships with others, and my writing. They've been two invaluable teachers to me.

Thanks to all who have given freely and generously of their time, expertise, experience, and technical information: Rena Schleifer, Ph.D.; Amy Kagedan, Ed.M.; Dan Sugarman, Ph.D.; Barbara Yasgur, M.D., O.T.R; Sarah Bingham, M.A.; Debbie Kramer, R.N., P.N.P.; Ann Bianchi; Valerie Sharfman; Mary Rose Mehorter of St. Joseph's School for the Blind; Merle Scott; Lee Bergman, director of Community Services at the Association for Retarded Citizens, Essex County, New Jersey; Dick and Norma Godin; Janice Vitiello; Cindy Reutsch, Family Support Services Coordinator of the New Jersey Association of the Deaf-Blind, Inc.; Vincent D'Agostino of the Association for Help of Retarded Children; Sue Lybolt of the Spina Bifida Association of America; and April Gimlin, chairperson of the United Ostomy Association Parents.

Thank you, Julia Banks, for your patience, support, and editorial skills.

I owe some of the creative and humorous chapter headings in this book to my sister, Valerie Sharfman, and her family, Jerome, Aubrey, Jill, Keith, Pamela, and Bern Sharfman.

Thank you, Sue and Neal Hecht, for your friendship, neighborliness, and child care.

Thank you, Bracha Trinz, Krystyna Orlowski, and Sue Hollar for your loving and creative child care while I wrote this book.

I'd like to express my appreciation to my wonderful family for their support: my in-laws, Mr. Harold and Mrs. Florence Yasgur; Rabbi Benjamin and Barbara Yasgur and their terrific children, Dr. Ezra and Sharie Sofair, and their adorable children as well.

Thanks to my mother, Mrs. Ruth Swift, for her clear, consistent parenting and love, for the honest relationship we enjoy, and for my first experience with toilet training!

Thanks to Kim and Jorge, two very special and challenging presences in our lives.

To my children, Mimi, Gila, Avi, and Leora—you guys are the greatest! Thanks for your energy, love, questions, support, and challenges.

Jordie: As always, you are my best friend, and *eizer k'negdi*. Your love and support encouraged me through this project, as through many others. I love you.

Last but not least, the memory of my father, Rabbi Isaac L. Swift, accompanies me always. I feel his presence (literary criticism, twinkling eyes, and warm support) whenever I write.

—BATYA SWIFT YASGUR

Contents

Foreword   xiii
Introduction   1

 1: Attitude   3
 2: The Process of Elimination   21
 3: Choosing a Potty   25
 4: Approaches to Toilet Training   35
 5: First Steps   51
 6: Good-bye Diapers!   69
 7: The One-Day Intensive Approach   77
 8: Toilet Training the Older Child   93
 9: General Tips   99
10: Defining and Preventing Bed-wetting   133
11: Encopresis (Fecal Soiling)   145
12: Special Situations   155
13: Stories   183

Oh, What a Relief It Is   193

Foreword

I'm so glad that Batya asked me to write this introduction, because with her request came a copy of the book. And what a wonderful book! It's so refreshing but all too rare that a book comes along that's well-written, brimming with uncommonly good sense, and yet full of compassion on this rather tender subject. By using some of the techniques described on a part-time basis over a period of two days my two-and-a-half-year-old little girl "decided" that she wanted to be toilet trained. My wife and I keep very busy with my practice so we didn't have time to use all of the suggestions. But the ideas we did try worked very, very well. It created a whole new perspective and atmosphere around the issue of toilet training that really helped my daughter and us to work together to get past this milestone with a minimum of hassle. By incorporating some of the ideas from the book, we all became much more conscious about the whole process. My daughter's physiology did respond to all of our intentions, and thus the deed was done. She has had but one accident since—while in the throes of a temper tantrum—but has otherwise been clean and dry, even at night! After using "Pull-Ups" for 10 days, just in case, she graduated to "big-girl" underwear with lots of fanfare and to the delight of us all.

If you're looking for accurate information and some ideas to help your little one make it into big girls' or big boys' pants, then THIS is *the* book to read and follow.

—JESSE A. STOFF, M.D.

Introduction

Congratulations! You're about to embark upon a wonderful, joyous journey with your child. You're about to experience the "joy of toilet training."

Perhaps you greet this with skepticism. You may be one of millions who regard toilet training as a difficult and lengthy process, one that is filled with stress and anxiety. Perhaps you've heard psychological myths suggesting that "poor toilet training" can ruin your child's emotional health. Well, here's good news for you. Toilet training does not have to be difficult or stressful. It does not have to be traumatic for you or your child. Toilet training can be a smooth, easy transition. It can even be fun!

This book will teach you how to make toilet training a time of shared learning for you and your child. It will introduce you to a number of different techniques. You can decide which are most appropriate for you and your child and design a toilet training program suited to your needs. Whether you are working outside your house or at home, whether you share parenting with a spouse or are a single parent, you will be able to create a plan that is most compatible with your life-style.

Techniques are invaluable tools toward accomplishing a

1

goal—in parenting or in any other area of life. But even more important than specific techniques is the attitude that accompanies them. This book will focus a good deal on attitude, because your attitude will spell the difference between experiencing toilet training as an ordeal, or experiencing it as a joyful challenge. Whatever technique you choose will be enhanced if you really enjoy what you're doing. You will be more effective, the process will be speedier, and most importantly toilet training will be a vehicle for greater closeness with your child.

So as not to favor or discriminate against either gender, I will be using the convention of s/he when referring to a child who could be either male or female. To enhance literary smoothness, as well as to personalize my remarks, I will often use proper names as well. If I am addressing an issue that concerns only boys, or only girls, I will state this explicitly.

Many psychologists now avoid the term "toilet training." They feel that "training" is something done with circus animals or pets, rather than with children. They prefer words like "teaching" or "learning" when referring to the process of helping a child to acquire toileting skills. While they are undoubtedly correct, I have decided to use "toilet training" because it remains the most popular term. This is, of course, no disrespect to the intelligence or unique humanness of a child. On the contrary: a primary focus of this book is helping parents to teach their children this important skill with love and respect.

Good luck! I wish you success and pleasure in the process!

1

Attitude

WHAT IS ATTITUDE, AND WHAT DOES IT HAVE TO DO WITH TOILET TRAINING?

Attitude can be defined as the internal stance that we adopt toward a person, situation, or idea. It's the sum of our feelings, thoughts, and beliefs at any given moment.

In any area of parenting, there are two factors that combine to form a course of action: attitude and techniques. Techniques are the actual steps taken. Attitude is the state of mind that accompanies those techniques.

In the case of toilet training, there are certainly many wonderful and useful techniques for a parent to learn. Indeed, many of your questions may have centered around such techniques. How shall I introduce the potty and what shall I say? Should I wait until my child asks to be trained or should I take the initiative by placing her/him on the potty? How many times a day and for how long? How should I handle it if my child balks and runs out of the bathroom?

These are valid and important questions, all of which will be addressed in the later chapters of this book. But first, let's discuss just how your attitude has an impact.

3

Why attitude is so important:

1) *You'll* feel better if you have a happy, positive attitude. If you regard toilet training (or any other aspect of parenting, for that matter) as a grim ordeal, that attitude is likely to become a self-fulfilling prophecy. You will probably experience the various components of toilet training (introducing the child to the potty, teaching her/him how to use it, dealing with the inevitable "accidents," and the occasional struggles and snags) as unfortunate and unpleasant. This means that you and your child are in for an unhappy experience.

2) *Your child* will feel better if your attitude is happy and positive. Children are remarkably intuitive, quick to perceive and react to their parents' moods and feelings. Parents—even those who are determined to hide their feelings—often betray themselves through their facial expressions, tone of voice, body language, or mannerisms. Parents who are not comfortable with their own feelings about toilet training are more likely to become irritable, impatient, and unsupportive of their children.

If this is the case, your child probably won't be very cooperative. Children crave encouragement and wholehearted support. A feeling of pleasure is far more likely to speed the process along than a feeling of dread.

3) Toilet training, like any other arena of parenting, holds out a wonderful opportunity for parents and children. It can be a shared venture of wonder and discovery, as you teach your child a new and important skill. Spending time with your child in the bathroom, applauding successes, showing yourself to be a warm and understanding presence in the face of accidents—all these are important ways to help bring you and your child closer.

So it's important to explore your beliefs and attitudes before you get started. This chapter is designed to help you get to know yourself a little better so that you can identify any attitudes that may interfere with the toilet training process. It will also give you some tips and pointers to help you make this a truly positive experience.

WHAT IF I DO SOMETHING WRONG?

Most new parents learn that people are quick to offer advice about all sorts of issues in child-rearing. Grandparents, aunts, uncles, friends, and even total strangers rush forward to make suggestions (and often offer criticisms) about feeding schedules, tantrums, sleeping problems, and disciplinary policies.

This is especially the case with toilet training. Everyone seems to have a different opinion about when to start and how to proceed. Some may feel strongly that a child who hasn't been trained by a year old will grow up to be undisciplined and pampered. They might still adhere to the school of thought that teaches that early training predisposes a child to neatness, cleanliness, and obedience.

Others who have been raised in the post-Freudian era have learned to regard toilet training as a tricky process, fraught with all sorts of psychological dangers. They may think parents can permanently scar their child's psychological development if they adopt the ''wrong'' approach and that their child will grow up to be neurotic.

The most modern research should be comforting to you. It points to a liberating conclusion: that there is basically no ''right'' or ''wrong'' approach in parenting. Any approach you choose has its advantages and disadvantages.

Like every other parenting decision, the approach to toilet training is a very personal one; there is no single ''right'' answer for all parents and all children.

Cross-cultural studies show a tremendous range of toilet training beliefs and practices. In Africa, for example, babies are trained quite literally from birth in a warm, natural, and easy-flowing way (see Chapter 4, "Approaches," for a more detailed discussion). They are already signaling their need to urinate or defecate well before their first birthday.

Is this method superior or inferior to the Western practice of putting babies in diapers and beginning to "train" them when they're older? It's neither superior *nor* inferior. Each culture and each family has its own life-style, rhythm, and personality. Again, what works for one will not necessarily be appropriate for the other. The most important thing is that the parents feel comfortable with themselves and their decision, whatever it might be; and that they implement any techniques, decisions, or policies with warmth, love, and acceptance of their child.

How can parents learn to be more comfortable? In a society like ours, which abounds in advice, criticism, and an often bewildering array of possibilities, how can parents choose a course of action and feel at ease with their decisions? And how can parents be loving and accepting of their child when s/he doesn't conform to all their wishes? The remainder of this chapter will explore these questions.

TRUST YOURSELF

From our earliest childhood, many of us have been taught to look outside ourselves for answers to our life situations. We have come to believe that others—teachers, doctors, psychologists, and other professionals—are the "experts" and know better than we do. This is especially true of parenting issues.

In her book *Every Child's Birthright*, Selma Fraiberg points out that non-Western cultures, wherever they may be located across the globe, all follow ancient traditions, in a natural, comfortable, and smooth-flowing way. Our culture, on the other hand, has devalued tradition as a valid and relevant path to follow and instead has encouraged parents to look to books and doctors for guidance. Thus parents today are left afloat with no anchor. They rely upon the most current scientific research to help them through the often bewildering process of child-rearing. But scientists don't always agree with one another as to what's best. What's more, ideas go in and out of vogue as scientists establish new trends, then debunk them in favor of yet newer (or older) ideas.

Perhaps it's time to suggest a novel approach: Look to yourself for answers. Parents have a more intimate knowledge of their child than any outsider could.

This doesn't mean that others might not have some interesting and important insights that may help in various predicaments you might face. Nor does it mean that books aren't valuable tools to help you understand yourself or your child better. It *does* mean that ultimately you know yourself and your child better than any outsider. Your own intuitions are probably more on target than those of others. Learn to trust yourself. If you want to start toilet training your child of three months using the from-birth approach outlined in Chapter 4, don't allow yourself to be dissuaded by pessimistic friends who believe you're out to traumatize your child for life. If you'd rather wait until your child is three years old and verbal, then trust yourself and your child.

If you feel unsure of yourself as a parent, then here are some questions you might want to ask yourself:

—In what types of situations do I feel unsure of myself? What is it about this situation that leads me to feelings of doubting myself and my own abilities as a parent?

—Are there certain people who seem to create within me feelings of self-doubt? Who are they? Why am I choosing to feel this way around them?

—If I feel unsure of myself because I'm a new parent with little experience, then am I using all available resources to acquaint myself with parenting ideas, issues, beliefs, and techniques? (Books, parenting classes, support groups, discussions with friends, relatives, and others who have experience with children?)

—Are there any issues lingering from my own childhood that are continuing to have an impact upon my feelings about my children?

DO YOU HAVE ANY BELIEFS ABOUT BATHROOM FUNCTIONS THAT MIGHT IMPINGE UPON TOILET TRAINING?

Excretion is a fact of life. It's neither good nor bad, neither clean nor dirty. True, wastes carry certain germs. For this reason, we get rid of them as quickly as possible. But people bring all sorts of beliefs to the bathroom that have nothing to do with simple hygiene.

When you're toilet training a child, a good deal of attention will be focused on excretion. After all, toilet training is all about excretion. If you're ill at ease with the subject, your child may sense your discomfort. This might be confusing to her/him.

What's more, your feelings of embarrassment about excretion may be absorbed by your child, then taken out of context. S/he may come to feel that something's wrong with *her/him*. For some children, the sense of shame becomes associated with the sexual organs, since they're so close in location to the excretory organs. This can have unfortunate repercussions later in life. So it's important to clarify your own feelings and beliefs about excretion before you begin training your child.

ISSUES OF GENDER

If you live in a two-parent household, or any living situation shared by men and women, it would be of great value to your child if both parents were involved with toilet training. Unfortunately, this isn't always the case. Some fathers actually boast that they've never changed a diaper since the baby was born!

Before you get started toilet training, discuss and coordinate your points of view. Whatever you decide—if Mom will do the training, while Dad sits on the sidelines—at least make sure you're both comfortable with that arrangement. If Dad will do the training while Mom washes her hands of the whole affair, make sure this is a clear, comfortable decision for both of you. If you're both planning to be involved, then be clear about this as well.

Here are some questions to help you clarify your roles:

—For men: Do I believe that it's inappropriate for men to be involved with "ladies' business" of diapering and toilet training? Why do I believe this? Do I believe that I, as a man, cannot train a little girl? Why do I believe that? If I am a single man training a daughter, are any issues coming up for me in connection with toilet training my little girl? Do I feel it would be helpful to have her trained by a woman? Why do I feel this way? Whom can I ask to help me?

—For women: Do I believe it's my job to train my child single-handedly without the help or involvement of the man in my life? If so, why do I feel this way? Do I believe that I, as a woman, cannot toilet train a little boy without the help of a man? Why do I believe that? How can I arrange for my son to watch other boys using the toilet?

—What will be our mutual roles in this endeavor?

YOUR FEELINGS ARE PRODUCTS OF CHOICE

Many of us have been taught that feelings happen upon us as we stand helplessly by. That we are the victims rather than the creators of our emotions. But, in truth, we choose our feelings. Each feeling we experience is the product of a belief, or a network of beliefs that we hold.

If you believe that your child can "make" you feel a particular way ("Jill, you wet your pants! You've made Mommy very sad." Or, "Kenny, you wouldn't sit on the potty! You've just made Daddy angry"), then you give her/him a tremendous amount of power. You're essentially giving up the responsibility for your own feelings and handing it over to a two-year-old! In fact, this type of dynamic underlies many power struggles between parents and children. Children love to feel like they're in control. They're not autonomous, and they are subject to the whims and fancies of the adults in charge in their lives—and often, they feel this acutely. These feelings can be addressed, of course, by giving your child as many choices as possible, within certain limits; and including her/him as much as possible in the decision-making process, even when the final say-so is yours.

The realization that, in the words of author Barry Neil Kaufman, "Happiness is a Choice" is a liberating and exhilarating one. It means that your state of mind can remain peaceful and happy, whether your child's underwear is wet or dry, and whether your child is cooperating or on strike. The happier you are, the happier and more cooperative your child is likely to be.

Here are some questions designed to help you explore your beliefs about happiness and unhappiness in general and parenting in particular.

—Am I a happy person? What do I mean by that?

—What types of situations, if any, lead to unhappy feelings in me? Why?

—Do I believe that others can make me unhappy or angry? Who? Do I believe my children can cause these feelings in me? How can they do this? Can I choose to feel otherwise? How can I accomplish this?

—If I feel unhappy, what is the reason? (Often the reason will be a belief such as, "If I weren't angry, my kids would never listen to me." Or "If I weren't unhappy, I'd never pursue what I want.") Can I maintain discipline in my children, or pursue my goals while remaining in an internal state of happiness and inner peace? How can I do this?

—How do I feel when my child doesn't listen to me? If I'm upset, why? How can I handle the situation without losing my emotional equilibrium and inner peace?

Barry Neil Kaufman's book *To Love Is to Be Happy With* is a wonderful handbook to help you uncover your beliefs and work with them to create a happier and more effective state of mind for yourself. Talking to a dear friend, a clergy member, a counselor, or other parents can also help to expand your view and your beliefs about parenting. The more flexible and easygoing you are, the more fun the process will be for you and your child.

DON'T JUDGE YOUR CHILD

When your child falls short of your ideals, it's a common reaction to fall into a state of judgmentalism and blame. "What you did was terribly wrong." "You're a bad boy." "You're a selfish little girl." "You're naughty." "You're immature and babyish." And on and on. Many of us as adults continue to hear echoes from our own childhoods of cutting, judgmental remarks hurled at us by our own parents in their anger.

But if we close our eyes and remember ourselves as

small children, we wonder: Were we really so terrible? Weren't we just being kids? Weren't we just doing the best we could at that time? Did we really deserve such harsh treatment?

According to Kaufman, nobody "deserves" to be blamed. We are all "trying the best we can" based on our beliefs. We are all on a common journey—we wish to be happy, we want the best for ourselves and our children.

Our children, too, are trying the best they can. Like little scientists, they are exploring their world, trying to see what will work for them, what will yield the results they want— their happiness.

Toilet training is an area that seems to elicit strong emotions in many parents. In fact, it is one of the leading causes for child abuse in this country! Many unresolved parenting issues or other areas of frustration can be played out in the toileting arena. For this reason it is crucial to get in touch with your own feelings and beliefs and clear up any lingering uncertainties.

Here are some questions to help you do this:

—Do I judge my child? How so, and in what circumstances do I find myself making judgments?

—When my child disobeys me, do I believe that s/he is deliberately thwarting me? Why do I see it that way? Is there some other way I could regard her/his disobedience? Have I acquainted myself with the age-appropriate behaviors of children? For example, two-year-olds are *known* to say "no" frequently. This doesn't mean they're "out to get you." One-year-olds often play with their food or spill their water to see what happens if they turn the cup upside down. This doesn't mean they're disrespectful toward food, nor that they want to see you do extra work. Certain behaviors simply are part of certain ages. Knowing this can make handling them a lot easier. If not, why? How could I do so now? (Talking to other parents, professionals, support groups, reading books, etc.)

—How can I realize my goals for my child (in this case, toilet training) without calling upon anger or judgmentalism as tools?

DISCIPLINE WITHOUT JUDGMENTS OR ANGER

Many parents feel that without anger, they'll never get their kids to listen to them. But this isn't really the case at all. *Discipline* comes from the same Latin root as *disciple*—which means student. To discipline someone doesn't mean to control or dominate. It means to teach and guide.

You can teach your child without anger in several ways:

1) Explain respectfully and clearly what you do and don't want. If your son wets his pants, explain in a clear and loving fashion why you don't want him to do so. You can do this even for a child who's a little too young to understand all the concepts.

2) Request that your child not do this again.

3) If your child continues to wet (and you feel this does not result from a medical problem, a lack of understanding, or a physical inability to remain dry), then you can give your child a natural consequence for his behavior: He has to help clean up the puddle, put the wet stuff in the laundry receptacle, and put on dry pants.

4) Screaming and anger tell the child only that s/he's worthless. Author Barry Neil Kaufman points out that ''how I [a parent] express my feelings is crucial. If I communicated what I wanted without anger, without fear, without threats . . . just stating that I wanted my possessions respected, my child could not leave my presence believing he was rejected or bad. It is only when I scream and call my child bad that I am telling him something global about himself. Often a child who has been punished or hit still feels and remembers the trauma of the attack long after he remembers the reasons why and the lesson behind it. In fact, the aggression is usually so frightening in its implications (of rejection and loss of love) that the child hardly hears the message. What he retains is the anger, the disliking, the message that he is 'bad.' '' (*To Love Is to Be Happy With*, pp. 67, 68.)

5) Screaming and anger may actually give the child a sort of reward. Children love action, intensity, and energy. This is why cartoon shows are so successful. When parents react with anger and fireworks, children often get a sort of thrill out of the performance, even though they're being yelled at. Some children relish any crumbs of attention from their parents, even if it takes the form of anger. So it's important to give your child the attention and thrills when s/he's doing what you want, not when s/he's disobeying you.

Even when your child doesn't completely carry out a desired chore, you can praise and acknowledge the part that s/he does perform. If Anne is willing to sit on the potty, but nothing "comes out," applaud her willingness to sit! If Kevin has started to wet his pants, but stopped himself and told you he needs the potty, then praise him for stopping himself and remembering to use the potty. Don't worry or start to think that then your child will never learn to do anything "right." The better s/he feels about her/himself, the more s/he will try to please you next time.

There is a charming little anonymously written poem about this:

> "Two A's are good!" the small boy cried.
> His voice was filled with glee.

His father answered with a shrug,
"Why didn't you get three?"

"Mom, I've got the dishes done!"
The girl called from the door.
Her mother very simply said,
"And did you sweep the floor?"

"I've mowed the lawn," the tall boy cried,
"And put the mower away."
His father blandly said to him,
"Did you clean off the hay?"

The children in the house next door
Seem happy and content.
The same things happened over there
But this is how they went.

"Two A's are good!" the small boy cried.
His voice was filled with glee.
His father answered with much joy,
"I'm glad you live with me."

"Mom, I've got the dishes done!"
The girl called from the door.
Her mother smiled at her and said,
"Each day I love you more."

"I've mowed the lawn," the tall boy cried,
"And put the mower away."
His father smiled at him and said,
"You've made my happy day."

Children need encouragement
For tasks they're asked to do.

If they're to lead a happy life,
So much depends on you!

When your child misbehaves, greet her/his actions with a bland and uninteresting response, as well as a civil explanation of why you don't like what s/he just did.

6) Occasional rewards can be wonderful ways of encouraging children and inviting them to listen to you. By this I don't necessarily mean material rewards—food treats or toys. A reward can be a rough-and-tumble tickle session, a piggyback ride, sitting down to read a book, going to the playground, or taking a walk together. Many parents who punish their children for misbehaving are nevertheless reluctant to reward their children for good behavior, lest they "spoil" them. They see a reward as a bribe.

But, as Barry Neil Kaufman points out, "A bribe comes from an unhappy or trapped state of mind; a trade or reward comes from a happy, clear state of mind." Giving your child something special to acknowledge your pleasure in her/his willingness to cooperate with you can be a wonderful boost to her/his self-esteem. It's just important not to allow rewards to substitute for praise, verbal appreciation, hugs and kisses.

If you find yourself unable to stay calm and loving when your child doesn't listen to you, then ask yourself the following questions:

—Why does it upset me when my child disobeys? Does this always happen, or only in certain circumstances? What are they? Why do these particular situations push my "buttons" and spark my anger?

—Is there something I'm afraid would happen if I weren't angry?

—What is most important to me? Getting what I want from my child, or remaining in a state of inner peace? Do

I believe I need to get what I want before I can feel peaceful and happy?

Do I praise my child when s/he listens to me? If not, why not? If so, is my praise really convincing and powerful in its delivery?

—Do I have certain beliefs about children and parents which might be contributing to my anger when my child disobeys me? (For example, if a child doesn't listen right away, s/he's defying her/his parents, and is unruly and out of control.) Why do I believe these things? Are these beliefs serving me now, in my relationship with my child?

—Are there techniques I can learn to cope with my anger if and when it does arise? Where can I find out more about these techniques? (There are some excellent books in the library about coping with anger—references follow at the end of the chapter. There are parenting support groups, national and local hot lines, friends, clergy and professional counselors to talk to.)

BE HONEST ABOUT YOUR FEELINGS

Recognizing that you choose your feelings doesn't mean denying them. If you're angry, then it's important to acknowledge your anger appropriately, and deal with it. If you're unhappy, upset, or disappointed in your child, then part of an honest parent-child relationship is sharing your feelings in a respectful but open fashion.

So if Mary has wet her dress for the seventh time today, and you *really* feel fed up, there's nothing wrong with your feelings, or with letting Mary know how you feel. But do so in a way that will honor her dignity. Don't say, ''Mary, you're the most impossible child! You've wet again! When will you learn to be clean and responsible?'' Rather say, ''Mary, I'm disappointed that you've wet yourself again.'' If Alan needs the bathroom five minutes after you've left the house for the airport, don't say, "You never listen to me! I told you to go to the bathroom, but you were too busy deciding which toys to pack in your suitcase! You're a selfish brat!" Instead say, "I'm angry because I asked you to use the bathroom and you refused. Finding a toilet now is very inconvenient!"

Psychologists call these "I" statements, because you're talking about yourself and your own feelings, rather than pointing an accusatory finger at your child. You're not making a global comment about her/him at all. Instead you're sharing your own feelings of disappointment, anger, or pain. You're also focusing on the incident at hand, rather than generalizing about your child's total worth as a human being.

Lastly, if you've lost your cool, then forgive yourself, recognize that you, too, are trying the best you can, and move on. Don't be afraid or ashamed to apologize honestly to your child. S/he will probably respect you all the more.

UNCONDITIONAL LOVE

Expressing pride in your child's accomplishments is wonderful and an excellent way to build your relationship with her/him, as well as her/his self-esteem. But don't lead your child to believe that your love is conditional and depends upon these accomplishments. Assure your child of your ongoing love, no matter what. Whether s/he uses the diaper or the potty to excrete, whether the underwear is wet or dry, your love for her/him is unwavering.

REFERENCES

Doty, Betty and Rooney, Pat. *Shake the Anger Habit.* Redding, CA: The Bookery, 1987.

Faber, Adele, and Mazlish, Elaine. *Liberated Parents, Lib-*

erated Children. New York: Avon Books, 1977.

Fraiberg, Selma. *Every Child's Birthright: In Defense of Mothering*. New York: Basic Books Inc., 1977.

Ginott, Haim. *Between Parent and Child*. New York: Macmillan, 1965.

Jampolsky, Gerald G. and Cirincione, Diane V. *Love Is the Answer: Creating Positive Relationships*. New York: Bantam Books, 1990.

Jampolsky, Gerald G. *Love Is Letting Go of Fear*. New York: Bantam Books, 1970.

Kaufman, Barry Neil. *To Love Is to Be Happy With*. New York: Ballantine Books, 1977.

Kaufman, Barry Neil. *Happiness Is a Choice*. New York: Random House, 1991.

Kaufman, Barry Neil. "No Risk/No Fault Parenting." An Option Process Tape, published by Option Indigo Press, 1987.

Mack, Alison. *Toilet Learning*. Boston, Toronto, and London: Little Brown and Company, 1977.

If you find yourself angry and fear that you may become abusive to your child, don't try to handle it alone! Contact a local mental health center, a friend, or clergyperson. Or call the Parents Anonymous Hot Line. It is set up to deal with concerns of abuse. You can reach them toll-free, anywhere in the United States, including Alaska and Hawaii at 1-800-421-0353.

2

The Process of Elimination— The Anatomy And Physiology of Excretion

An amusing comparison can be made between the human being and the computer. You feed both with input, listen to a few gurgling noises, and wait for output to appear at the other end. But how does this work? What happens inside the body that ultimately produces wastes? Obviously a complete and detailed answer to this question would become a complicated medical treatise, far beyond the scope of this book. But some understanding of the process of elimination can be useful in gaining insight into the act of toileting. It can also help you to be more easygoing with your youngsters, by helping you realize that the organs and muscles involved are maturing. These internal pieces of equipment will take time before they reach the same degree of control as those of an adult.

Urine is stored in the bladder, a pear-shaped organ with an elastic wall. When the bladder is full, urine passes through the urethra and is released. Bowel movements are stored in the large intestine and are released through the rectum.

The bladder as well as the rectum are kept closed by a set of circular muscles called sphincter muscles. When the bladder or rectum feels full, the sphincter muscles open, thereby releasing the stored contents.

Under ordinary circumstances, adults can control their sphincter muscles. They can recognize the sensation of a full bladder or rectum, and can consciously tighten their muscles to hold back excretion until they reach the appropriate location. Then they can consciously relax their sphincter muscles to allow the excreta to pass. In adults, these are called voluntary muscles.

In a baby, however, these are involuntary muscles. The baby is not aware of the sensation of fullness and cannot consciously hold back urine or bowel movements. When an infant eats, the entire gastrointestinal tract activates to digest the food in the stomach and process wastes. The sphincter muscles relax, and a movement ensues. The liquid taken in with breast milk or formula increases the volume of stored fluid in the bladder, and the baby urinates. (Most parents have noted that their baby often produces a bowel movement during nursing or immediately afterward and almost invariably is wet as well.)

As children mature, their digestive tract also matures. The child becomes increasingly aware of the sensations that accompany elimination—the "need to go," and then the act of releasing. Usually this begins to happen close to the child's first birthday. By the time children are about a year and a half old, they've begun to take note of their excretory process—especially defecation. Chapter 5, "First Steps," will teach you how to heighten that awareness in your child, thereby speeding the process along.

Your child's bladder and intestinal capacity are also growing, so urine or stool can be retained for longer periods of time. Most children seem to follow a pattern in their ability to retain:

1) The child first becomes able to retain bowel movements while asleep;

2) The child retains movements during most waking hours;

3) The child retains urine while awake;

4) Lastly, the child learns to retain urine while asleep.

Of course, these processes don't happen automatically—they need your help and guidance through the toilet training process.

It is important to realize that the digestive system is not fully mature even in later childhood. Children are more prone than adults to occasional "accidents"—when they are excited or disturbed, or when they've drunk too much and not taken the time to go to the bathroom. As the child develops, her/his digestive system develops, too, and eventually these problems are left behind.

Many factors can affect the digestive system in children (and in adults, too, for that matter). Diet has a profound impact on excretion. (This is discussed at length in Chapter 9, "General Tips," section on Constipation. A diet rich in fats, sugars, refined flours, and other "junk" foods, and deficient in fruits, vegetables, whole grains, and other fibers will have a deleterious effect upon digestion. Certain food additives, as well as other common allergens can have an impact upon urination as well as defecation. You would do well to feed your child a diet high in chemical-free, natural foods.

Stress is a second prime offender. Adults as well as children often respond to stressful situations with digestive disturbances. This book will suggest several ways to handle stress if you believe it's affecting your child's toileting.

Some medications have side effects that disturb urinary or bowel patterns. If your child is on any medication, always remember to check with your pediatrician and ascertain whether excretion will undergo any changes. By this I don't necessarily mean exotic medications used to treat rare diseases. Even a medication as commonplace as antibiotics may produce nausea, diarrhea, and other digestive changes. Familiarize yourself with these possibilities *before* they become an issue.

Your doctor or pediatric nurse is an excellent resource. It's important for you to feel comfortable asking any questions you have about elimination (or any other subject, for that matter). They can help you understand better what's happening, and address themselves to specific concerns.

3

Choosing a Potty

The most important piece of equipment you'll need in toilet training is, of course, the potty. Here are some guidelines and suggestions.

WHY DO WE NEED A POTTY?

Most child care experts today recommend starting toilet training by using a potty rather than a toilet. There are several reasons for this.

1) *Adult toilets are awfully big!* To a small child, an adult toilet may be somewhat intimidating. Consider how high it is, in comparison with your child's height. Consider how wide the bowl is, in comparison with your child's little bottom. Now imagine yourself trying to sit on a toilet designed for giants, where your feet don't touch the ground, and you have to balance yourself precariously on the edge of an enormous bowl, many times your size. You might also feel a bit put off by the prospect. One of the things you definitely *don't* want in toilet training is to have your child too frightened to use the necessary equipment. A small, child-sized potty is far less likely to generate fear in your child.

2) *The water sure looks deep in there!* Your child may also be somewhat frightened by the deep water in the toilet bowl or the noise the toilet makes when flushed. Both of these concerns are, of course, eliminated with the potty.

3) *"I can do it all by myself!"* An important goal of toilet training is to teach your child independence. A child can independently climb onto and off a potty, but will need assistance in getting on and off the toilet. If you are training an older child, of course, s/he can use a stepladder to reach the toilet. But for younger children, and even for some older children, a potty is a greater invitation to independence than a toilet.

4) *"Mom, Dad, watch me!"* You also want your child to develop a sense of self-confidence and self-assurance. Again, a sturdy potty that can be mastered alone is far more likely to build self-confidence than an adult toilet that requires parental assistance.

5) *"Just like Mom and Dad."* Most children love child-sized versions of adult items. If you're sweeping, they'll be thrilled to sweep, too, with a little broom. If you're writing at your desk, they'll be delighted to scribble with a crayon at their little desk. They'll probably be equally tickled to have their own little toilet.

6) *The family "bathroom hour."* Because imitation is such an important part of toilet training (see Chapter 5, "First Steps"), your child may be spending quite a bit of time in the bathroom watching others use the toilet. If Jane is so inspired, it's helpful for her to have her own little potty handy to try out being "just like Mommy or Daddy." If there are older siblings, you can suggest a joint "bathroom hour," in which the older sibling sits on the toilet, while the smaller child sits on the potty. You can suggest a contest to see who will make first, or any other motivational ploys that might come to mind. But you can only do so if you have a separate potty for your child.

7) *A potty is portable.* Some parents prefer to train their child in the kitchen or den, or any other room that is most in use. (See Chapter 5, "First Steps.") They feel it's more convenient to have an easily accessible potty, so that they can watch their toddler while they get other work done. Obviously, they can't move a toilet around the house. And even if you feel that elimination is an activity that should be confined to the bathroom, there may be occasions when a movable potty will be a blessing. For example, if your house is crowded with guests, and the bathroom is in heavy use, you may decide to move the potty somewhere else for those few days. When you travel, it's mighty convenient to carry a potty with you. (See Chapter 9, "General Tips," discussion of Traveling.) The potty makes all these options available to you.

8) *It's healthier for your child to have her/his feet planted solidly on the ground.* There is a physiological reason why the potty is preferable to the toilet. When a child bears down to push out a bowel movement, having her/his feet on the floor allows the necessary leverage to do so without straining the anal muscles. (In countries that don't have modern plumbing, people squat, using a variety of muscles, plus the force of gravity, to aid in the expulsion of their movements.) A child whose feet are dangling might come to rely too heavily upon anal muscles to do the job.

Of course, that situation can be remedied by a large footstool. If you decide to train your child directly onto the toilet, you will need to get a stool or stepladder until s/he is tall enough to reach the floor.

9) *Won't I have to train my child twice?* Some parents are concerned that if they begin the toilet-training process by using a potty, they'll then have to train their child all over again to use the toilet. But it really doesn't work that way. The most important aspect of toilet training is teaching your child restraint and postponement. In other words, Sally must restrain herself from wetting or soiling diapers or underwear; and she must postpone production until she reaches the vessel in the bathroom and is sitting upon it. Once that concept has been grasped and incorporated into your child's behavior, she should be able to apply it to the toilet as well as the potty.

Some parents are concerned that their children will refuse to use a toilet when traveling if they are accustomed to the potty. But if the possible toilet fears are dealt with, and if your child is used to visiting many different toilets (see Chapter 5, "First Steps"), s/he will probably be willing to try out a toilet when no potty is available. You can further that end by portraying the toilet as an exciting new adventure, and also by buying a toilet seat adaptor (see below). If your child is really unwilling and unready to try the big toilet, then continue to travel with a potty for a while. Wait a few months, then try again. (Traveling with a potty is a pretty good idea anyway—see Chapter 9, "General Tips.") As your child grows taller and more confident, as toilet training becomes second nature, s/he will probably be willing to expand her/his horizons and try out the toilet.

For further tips, see Chapter 9, "General Tips"—"The Transition from Potty to Toilet."

WHAT KIND OF POTTY SHOULD I CHOOSE?

Of course, as with so many other aspects of toilet training, there are no "shoulds," no iron-clad rules and regulations that must be followed. Here, however, are a few helpful suggestions.

1) *Sturdy and Steady.* Any potty you choose should be sturdy and steady. In order to ensure that your potty will

remain firmly on the floor, even if your child sometimes squirms around, make sure that the bottom is somewhat wider than the top. Have your child sit on it in the store and make sure it won't tip over when your child moves, or if someone's foot accidentally bumps into it. A child who falls off the potty may be considerably more reluctant to use it again.

2) *Armrests are not the best idea.* Some potties are shaped like ordinary chairs and even have armrests. These armrests can contribute to the potty's toppling over. Your child may grab one side and use it to help her/himself climb up, thereby creating an imbalance and toppling the whole thing onto its side.

3) *Potties that are also high chairs.* Some potties double as high chairs. They are designed so that you can feed your child and s/he can engage in elimination at the same time. This might be confusing to your child and convey an erroneous message: that eating is the time for defecation. You don't really want your child to learn that the table is the place for waste production. You want to communicate a clear and consistent message about when and where elimination is to take place.

4) *Potties with trays.* Some potties come with trays. The idea is that a child should have a place to organize toys, books, or snacks while sitting on the potty. This is supposed to increase motivation to sit longer and try harder to make.

The problem is that the tray impedes easy access to the chair. Furthermore, the toys often distract children from the business at hand. (See Chapter 5, "First Steps" for a more complete discussion of the use of toys to occupy your child while on the potty.) And for reasons discussed above, the bathroom is not the place for snacks. If your potty comes with a tray, make sure it's one that you can detach. And if you *do* decide to allow playing while on the potty, then a single toy or book will suffice, and can be held without a tray.

5) *Remove those straps.* Some potties come with straps, designed to restrain the child and keep her/him in place. It seems that these are holdovers from the time when it was believed that children had to sit until they made a bowel movement, no matter how long it took. There is no place for such restraining devices in the toilet training process. If your potty is sturdy and firm, and your child is developmentally ready to sit unaided, then there should be no fear of falling off. If not, then get another potty, or wait until your child is older before beginning. What's more, when your child is ready to get up, s/he will stand up in spite of the straps and drag the potty around like a cumbersome tail. It will be uncomfortable, perhaps even painful. It'll also be quite unsanitary, if there's anything in the potty.

6) *Potties with music boxes.* Some potties come with music boxes that play a melody each time the child deposits a movement or urinates into them.

In some models, the music box is located behind the seat. Your child will probably twist around to investigate the box and be distracted from concentrating on bodily functions.

7) *Animal potties.* Some potties have animal figures sticking up prominently in front. The child climbs on and straddles the potty, as s/he would straddle a toy horse at the carousel. For some children, it creates difficulties in climbing up themselves, and they need someone to help them, thereby defeating the goal of helping your child reach maximum independence as soon as possible.

8) *The deflector cup.* Most potties come with splatter cups designed to prevent little boys from spraying their urine all over the room. Make sure the potty you get has a detachable cup, because you'll probably want to get rid of it. Many children—boys and girls—have scraped themselves on the cup. Depending on how it's positioned, it might press into your child's groin. It also keeps you from peering between your child's legs and checking whether or not urination is taking place. So put away the deflector when you get the potty. And don't worry about urine spraying all over the place. Little boys can be taught to aim their penis downward into the potty. And although most little boys start learning to urinate by sitting down, some stand up right away. It's a game for a child to aim and see if he can get it into the potty.

9) *Potties with detachable seats.* Some potties come with detachable seats. The idea is that once the child gets older, you can remove the seat from the potty and use it as a toilet seat adaptor. It's a great idea. Just make sure that the seat removes easily, and that you and your spouse don't need advanced training in engineering to figure out how to do it.

10) *Keep a lid on!* A potty with a lid has several advantages. One is that it confines odors more than an unlidded potty. As your child gets older and more independent, s/he may wander into the bathroom and use the potty when you're busy with something else. While some child care experts believe that children should be responsible for dumping the potty themselves (see Chapter 5, "First Steps" for a more complete discussion), others feel that this places an unnecessary burden on the child, and that it's sufficient for the child to use the potty appropriately. If you feel this way, then there might be some time lapse between your child's use of the potty and your arrival to clean it out. During that time, a lid will help to limit the odor.

11) *Make sure your potty leaves room for growth.* When you're at the store, trying out different potties, have your child sit on them. Project what s/he will look like, say, a year from now. Some children use the potty until they're in nursery school. So you want to leave plenty of room for growth.

12) *The potty as a "little toilet."* Some potties are shaped like miniature toilets. Because so many children love to have miniature versions of adult items, and because imitation is such an important part of toilet training, these are excellent potties to obtain.

13) *A removable bowl.* A potty with a removable bowl is much easier to clean than one with a permanently attached bowl. The bowl's contents can be dumped into the toilet by you or your child and washed clean over the sink or tub. Make sure the bowl can be removed easily by little fingers if you decide that this is a responsibility that you'd like your child to assume.

WHY USE A TOILET SEAT ADAPTOR?

You might decide not to use a potty, but to train your child straight onto the toilet. Perhaps you have a tiny bathroom, with no room for a potty to stand on the floor. Whatever your reason, a toilet seat adaptor is preferable to the adult toilet seat alone. Here's why:

1) Fears: Your child might be afraid of falling into this big, watery hole. The toilet seat adaptor makes the hole smaller and more manageable, so your child can relax on it without the fear of falling in.

2) *Some children have difficulty balancing themselves.* It's quite an act of acrobatics and balancing for a little toddler to learn to hold onto a grown-up toilet seat without falling in.

3) The toilet seat adaptor is excellent for helping in the transition between potty and toilet.

DIFFERENT TYPES OF ADAPTORS

There are many different types of adaptors available. Look for durability, safety, and comfortable fit. If something feels flimsy, then don't buy it. If it's wooden, make sure it won't splinter. And be sure it leaves room for your child to grow, without being so enormous that your child risks falling into the toilet.

Adaptors with steps are excellent, because they enable your child to climb up without help. This leads to a sense of independence and pride in her/his accomplishments. It also makes the distance between the potty and the floor seem a little less formidable. The steps are important, too, because they provide a resting place for your child's feet while pushing out bowel movements. This takes the strain off the anal muscles.

Many stepladder toilet seat adapators provide handles for the child to hold while sitting on the toilet. These are excellent. Children are often concerned that they might fall off the toilet. The handles give them a sense of security.

If your adaptor comes with a deflector, then remove it. For the same reasons as it wasn't desirable or necessary in the potty, it's not desirable or necessary in the adaptor either. Anyway, by the time your little boy is ready to use the toilet, he will probably be ready to learn how to stand up when he urinates.

Make sure the adaptor you buy fits all toilet seats. Some won't fit onto odd-sized commercial toilets or padded toilet seats. Some adaptors are more versatile than others. Try a few out, read packages carefully, and see which works best.

There is one excellent stepladder adaptor on the market that is a potty as well as an adaptor. It can be arranged so as to stand on the floor and serve as a potty. If you remove the bowl and turn it around, it becomes a stepladder adaptor for the toilet. If your funds or space are limited, and you're planning to buy a single unit that will serve all your child's needs throughout the toilet training process, then this is probably the best item on the market for your needs.

There is a folding adaptor on the market as well. This is super for travel, because it folds neatly and compactly. It'll fit into a large pocketbook, a diaper bag, or a small valise. You can easily carry it with you into department stores, malls, libraries, or any other public area. It's more sanitary to have your child sit on your own seat than on the public one. It may also be reassuring for your child to have this familiar object in a large, alien bathroom.

If you have a tiny apartment, with little room to store a potty or even a stepladder adaptor, the folding toilet seat may be the answer for you. It's so compact, you can store it anywhere.

CLEANING YOUR POTTY

Most potties need to be simply emptied and rinsed after each use. You might want to wipe the interior clean with a paper towel or rag to remove any vestiges of urine or feces that might remain. An occasional washing with baking soda should keep odors from forming.

4

Approaches to Toilet Training

Okay. Now you know about the internal processes that lead up to a wet or soiled diaper. You've examined and explored some of the beliefs and feelings that come up for you in connection with parenting in general, and toilet training in particular. As a result of these explorations, you're loving, accepting, and eager to begin the exciting voyage on which you're about to embark with your child. The question is: What approach to use?

This chapter will outline some of the basic approaches to toilet training. It will discuss advantages and disadvantages of each approach, and help you decide which approach is best for *you* and your child. Remember that nothing is written in stone. These are not a set of divinely revealed dogmas, nor are they the last word in scientific knowledge laid down by some group of "experts" in their ivory towers. These are practical guidelines, the result of collective parenting wisdom and psychological research. You are the best expert on which approach will be most suited to your family and child. You can adapt, modify, combine and play with all the ideas presented in this chapter (and indeed, throughout the book) until you come up with a series of steps that are tailor-made for your particular situation and your child's.

LAISSEZ-FAIRE (ALSO KNOWN AS NO TOILET TRAINING AT ALL)

Some parents adopt a completely laissez-faire attitude. They believe that the best way to train a child is *not* to train her/him at all. When s/he is ready, s/he will independently initiate training and will "train her/himself."

There are certainly some children who "get the hang of it" without actually being taught anything, and who are naturally neat, clean, and self-motivated. In an atmosphere of total trust and love, such children can do fine with this approach. Trusting your child is something that must emanate from a completely and totally comfortable internal stance. If you feel the slightest doubt, your child will feel mistrusted and confused.

Some children, too, are simply not interested in the toilet, no matter how much they're trusted. This often accounts for enuresis or encopresis in older children. (See Chapters 8 and 11, "Toilet Training the Older Child" and "Encopresis.") They may find themselves at age four or five suddenly in a pressure situation, in which parents or others are desperate to have them trained, and in which the sense of trust in their autonomy is suddenly revoked.

So in most situations, it's better to be involved in a teaching process, rather than to sit back and hope your child will catch on by her/himself. Teaching ideally should always respect the freedom and individuality of the person taught—whether child or adult. The various methods put forth in this book are designed to promote a respectful, joyous experience of toilet training, which trusts the child's natural desire to learn, and the child's own pace and style.

TOILET TRAINING FROM BIRTH

The concept of toilet training from birth may raise many eyebrows, especially in our Western culture. It sounds alien and unrealistic, given the nature of a tiny infant. It also raises the hackles of those who are psychologically educated, who associate this notion with the coercive methods used to toilet train young infants during the early part of this century.

It's true that in the early 1900s, toilet training *did* begin at birth. The United States government publication *Infant Care* recommended that parents (correction: "mothers") begin bowel training immediately after birth. The revised 1929 edition advised beginning at one month. "The mother should hold him over the chamber lap potty, using a soap stick, if necessary, to start the movement, and continue day after day, not varying the time by five minutes, until the baby is fixed in this habit."

Bladder training was dealt with more leniently. Mothers were advised to wait until the third month, but no longer. "In order to be effective, the chamber must be presented to the baby at the same hour every day, usually just before the morning bath, and it must be presented persistently until the habit is formed. Much time and patience will be required on the part of the mother."

The atmosphere of this training was rigid and harsh. Babies old enough to sit were placed on a potty and strapped there until they made. One gets a grim impression of the mother as sergeant major, standing sternly over a squirming toddler, who's more eager to crawl and explore than to sit and excrete, ordering her/him to excrete OR ELSE!

Child care "experts" of those days believed that children were innately disorderly beings, and the primary job of the mother was to create orderly habits. Those habits would ultimately produce a well-disciplined, well-behaved child. They believed that holding a crying baby for too long could "spoil" her/him, and that parents should never play with their babies. Feedings, baths, and toileting were inflexibly scheduled. A child who learned to excrete in the potty, and on schedule, would develop habits of regularity, "cleanliness, and delicacy."

There were other odd beliefs that contributed to the pressure to toilet train early. Doctors had a notion that bulky diapers would lead to deformities of the thigh. Doctors were also afraid that unexcreted fecal material, if allowed to remain in the intestines, would be reabsorbed into the body, spreading poisons throughout the system. Both these concepts are entirely erroneous from a medical point of view, but while they were accepted, they fueled the movement for early toilet training.

Toilet training was seen not only as a means of keeping a child clean, healthy, and dry, but also as a means of establishing parental control. Parents were encouraged to place children on the potty or toilet whether they needed to relieve themselves or not, just to establish authority.

Additionally, the burden on mothers was tremendous. They had none of our modern labor-saving devices, disposable diapers, or diaper services. Nor did they have the support and task-sharing of tribal societies, where the women share responsibilities and work as groups. Families were large, with many small children following in quick succession. The volume of scrubbing, boiling, and folding must have been enormous. It's no wonder that mothers were eager to get their children out of diapers as soon as possible.

On the other hand, Sigmund Freud, pioneer and father of modern psychology, railed against the harsh toilet training methods of his time. He felt that excessively rigid toilet training could lead to psychological and emotional problems in later life. Psychologists and other child care experts, following suit, began to take a more lenient approach to toilet training. Early training fell into disrepute. It was felt that a child is not ready to be trained until approximately two and a half years old. By this time, the child is intellectually capable of understanding what is required; is able to communicate the need to use the potty; and has the sufficient sphincter control to hold in urine and feces until s/he gets there. Parents are now being discouraged from training their children too early.

While it's certainly true that the child's sphincter muscles are still not fully mature during the first and second year, that doesn't mean that these muscles are completely useless, and can't be effectively employed in learning toileting skills early. Children *can* learn the necessary steps to toileting long before they're two and a half. The key lies in the attitude.

Cross-cultural studies show that many children in non-Western, "primitive" societies are toilet trained well before they're a year old. In his book *Toilet Training Without Tears,* Charles Schaeffer describes children of the African Digo tribe and how they are trained. Interestingly, children of the Yequana and Sanema tribes of South America are trained in an almost identical fashion. This is described at length in Jean Liedloff's book *The Continuum Concept.* The approach is loving, nurturing, and natural.

It evolves from the life-style of non-Western, non-modern societies, in which the mother carries her child in a soft baby carrier all the time. (In her book *Every Child's Birthright,* Selma Fraiberg points out that Western mothers are the only ones to use cribs, cradles, plastic infant seats, strollers, and so on in transporting their babies. Tribal mothers—whether from Africa, Asia, South America, or Australia—carry their babies on their persons.) The babies also sleep in the same bed with their mothers. In other words, the mother and the baby are in constant bodily contact twenty-four hours a day from the moment the child is born. (When the child is several months old, siblings and others are granted the privilege of carrying the baby as well.)

After a couple of days, the mother becomes completely in tune with her baby's body rhythm and signals. She knows when her child is about to wet or soil, and removes her/him from the baby carrier. She positions the baby at a comfortable angle over an appropriate location on the ground and allows her/him to carry out her/his business there. Thus the child learns from the very beginning that there is a particular position and location for eliminating wastes. Unlike Western babies, who wet or soil wherever they happen to be because they wear a diaper that will contain their wastes, these babies learn that one must go someplace else to make.

By the time they are old enough to signal for anything—to gesture, grimace, point, or make noises—they are already signaling when they need to relieve themselves. Then their mother, or a sibling, takes them to the appropriate place.

When I was in the Rutgers School of Social Work, I had an Indian classmate who had been toilet trained in that fashion. She told me that when she read our various textbooks dealing with toilet training, she called her mother in India and had a good laugh. Her mother told her that she had been trained by six or seven months old, and so had all her family members for generations.

There are some American mothers who, inspired by *The Continuum Concept,* are attempting to live a more "natural" life-style, carrying their babies in baby carriers by day, and allowing them to sleep in their beds at night. It is, however, still difficult for these mothers to intuit their babies' body signals and potty them accordingly. Why? Perhaps it's because the American life-style has more distractions than a native life-style. We have televisions, radios, computers, airplanes, and cars—just to name a few items that are unknown in non-modern societies. It is more difficult to be in tune with subtle signals when our attention is so easily engaged by so many forms of stimulation. So the toilet training from birth alternative is more difficult for us in our society to adopt.

Dr. Charles Schaeffer outlines a second toilet training from birth alternative (*Toilet Training Without Tears*):

1) Purchase a lap potty. This looks like a giant bowl or teacup. It should ideally be made out of porcelain, metal, or hard plastic, because these materials don't retain odors as easily as soft plastic. Lap potties aren't always so easy to come by, so you might have to use your own ingenuity and buy a basin or something else for the purpose. It helps if the potty has a lip, so that it won't fall through your legs and onto the floor. Make sure it doesn't have any sharp edges that might hurt your child. Make sure, too, that the potty isn't so big that your little baby's buttocks will fall right in.

2) Keep the lap potty and toilet paper or baby wipes at your side when your infant is feeding;

3) Undo the baby's diaper for easy access (if s/he's nursing from your left breast, then the left diaper tab should be opened, and vice versa. If you bottle-feed, then determine which side you usually cradle her/him—let's say the right side—and open her/his diaper on the right tab).

4) Be alert to your baby's body signals, and observe carefully. You might want to take several days for observation before you actually begin. Take note of whether there's a tightening of the belly, heavier or slower breathing, straining or other noises when defecating.

5) Once you've acquainted yourself with your child's

body language of elimination, you're ready to begin. As soon as you observe the telltale signs, immediately remove the diaper (since it's open on one side, you can use one hand) and place the potty under the buttocks. Position the potty on your lap between your legs, and lean the baby against your chest and belly, with her/his bottom over the potty.

6) Make sure to cover the front of the baby, not just the back, to prevent being sprinkled, especially if it's a boy.

7) Replace your baby in the crook of your arm and resume feeding.

8) Leave the potty in place until the feeding has ended.

9) Use the toilet paper or wipes to clean up anything that might have been produced.

10) If nothing has been produced, don't worry! Refasten the diaper, and try again later.

11) Keep observing your baby even when it's not feeding time, and when you notice the telltale body signs, set her/him on the potty, on your lap, in the position described.

12) Check diapers frequently. When a diaper has been dry for a longish period of time (say, half an hour to an hour), bring out the potty and place it under your child.

13) Keep track of your child's elimination times. Dr. Schaeffer has a sample schedule in his book.

14) Place the child on the potty regularly. Once s/he can sit independently, allow her/him to do so regularly.

15) Praise your child for sitting on the potty. And enthusiastically praise every time urination or defecation occurs.

As your child matures, you can help her/him to initiate pottying her/himself. Dr. Schaeffer calls this "Self-Initiated Toileting," and advises a series of steps beginning with reaching for the potty and then grabbing it when the child feels the need to go. This addresses the concern that it is the parent, rather than the child, who is toilet trained. In other words, when a parent is trained to "catch" the child's movements, it is the *parent*, not the child, who has been trained. The child is merely the passive recipient of the parent's wishes. Dr. Schaeffer's suggested program is a way of actively involving even a young baby in the process.

There are several advantages of the early approach:

1) If finances are a problem for you, then every diaper saved is a valuable savings in money. This early approach means that a fair number of movements and urinations will land in the potty, consequently saving that number of diapers. As the child grows older, s/he will need fewer and fewer diapers.

2) There is a great possibility (though it won't necessarily happen this way) that your child will be pretty well trained by age eighteen months—a great savings in money and convenience for you.

3) Your children become accustomed to toileting as a routine and are less likely to balk at it than if you initiate it at a later stage.

4) Your child becomes accustomed to using the potty for elimination, therefore eliminating in a diaper doesn't feel quite right. Her/his earliest consciousness is that the potty is the natural place to take care of this.

5) It's a fun and interesting experiment in seeing how early you can teach your baby to do something—again, if you approach it with a nonjudgmental, noncoercive attitude, and without unrealistic expectations.

There are, however, several disadvantages to toilet training from birth.

1) It seems like an extremely complicated and cumbersome process, requiring intense concentration and parental involvement, extensive record-keeping, and a good deal of hovering. American parents are not African or South American tribal mothers. The demands and complexities of our American culture make the natural, simple method used by the Digo in Africa virtually impossible for us. The process involves a level of commitment and involvement that exceeds that of our African counterparts.

2) Not only is this approach more time-consuming in terms of the number of hours per day spent in toileting the baby, but it's also more time-consuming in terms of the number of months the whole process will take. An older child will take anywhere between a few weeks (for a few lucky parents) and a few months to complete training. In contrast, a child who begins training before s/he reaches five months of age is likely to take at least ten months to become trained—possibly longer.

3) It's altogether too easy, in this highly competitive society in which we live, to fall into the ''superbaby'' trap. Some parents, perhaps believing that their children will acquire the competitive edge over other children, are teaching their babies to read, do mathematics, and all sorts of other things. For such parents, this might become an additional arena for ''superizing'' their baby. They may place too much pressure on the baby and respond with judgments and disappointment when the baby fails to live up to their unrealistic standards. This may bring unnecessary suffering to the baby (and the parents, for that matter) and leave long-term emotional scars.

4) Periods of regression are more likely, because younger children tend to be more forgetful than older children.

5) Not all babies defecate neatly and predictably on schedule. Some are quite irregular. It's not uncommon for some infants to pass a bowel movement every couple of days, while others do so a few times a day. Trying to figure out a schedule may be next to impossible.

6) You may be traveling, or be going through a particularly busy period of time, which will make it difficult to keep a potty on hand at all times and to carefully observe the minutiae of your child's body language.

7) Your baby-sitter, or other family members who may spend time with your child, may not want to exercise the vigilance necessary if you're going to catch your child's movements before they come out. They also may not be as keenly aware of your child's body language as you are. This means that you'll either have to suspend the training during those times when your child is with other people—which may be confusing to your child, and will send her/him mixed signals about where to pee and poop—or you'll have to be around her/him full-time. This may be inconvenient to you; not to mention the feeling that so many mothers often develop of being "trapped." It's important, even for the most devoted parents, to be able to have some time away from their children—to relax, take a walk, engage in recreation, and so on—and creating a situation that will cement you to your child may not be the most desirable state of affairs.

8) If you are still struggling with your attitude, if you tend to become tense, impatient, angry, or judgmental, then the frequent episodes of "missing" your child's movements may be frustrating to you, and you may come to take out your feelings on your child.

9) Some parents feel comfortable and natural holding an infant. For them, bottle-feeding or nursing the baby doesn't require a massive effort in coordination and a deep level of concentration. Many other parents—mothers and fathers—have little experience with infants. They feel awkward and clumsy when holding a baby, especially at the beginning. It takes them time to begin to feel comfortable adjusting the position of the baby during a feeding. (Many hospitals offer breast-feeding classes for this reason.) Trying to set up a lap potty during a feeding (and don't forget, the baby is leaning on one arm, so you have to do it one-handed) may entail a major balancing act. This could add extra and unnecessary stress to an already challenging experience.

So all in all, exercise your own good sense, and your own self-awareness to determine the appropriateness of this approach for you. And remember, nothing is written in stone. If you venture into this one, and it doesn't work out for you, don't blame yourself or your baby. Let go of it, and try one of the other approaches described below.

THE ONE-YEAR-OLD VERSUS THE TWO-YEAR-OLD

Early toilet training—beginning close to a child's first birthday (say, nine to fourteen months)—has fallen into disrepute for the same reasons as toilet training from birth. Because this was such a common approach, and because it was associated with the rigidity and harshness that used to abound in the pre-psychological era, many of today's child care experts advise parents to steer clear of it.

There are, however, quite a few advantages to beginning early—IF your attitude is relaxed, loving, and warm.

1) If you begin shortly after your child has learned how to sit independently for a nice stretch of time (your child will probably be between six months to a year or so), then your child sees sitting as a novelty. S/he often regards each new accomplishment as a sort of new toy to be played with until it loses its excitement. Most children are eager to show off their new skill and will be delighted to sit on chairs, floors, couches—and potties.

2) One-year-olds are usually eager to please. They're

highly social beings who delight in being tickled, played with, and applauded. If they see that you enjoy what they're doing, they'll probably be only too glad to repeat the performance. You can use this trait to your advantage, and applaud their willingness to sit on the potty and any production that may ensue.

3) Two-year-olds are often "no-sayers." (See Chapter 9, "General Tips".) They're testing their wings a little, trying to push their limits, and are not known for their cooperativeness. Quite the contrary, if you begin the training process *before* your child turns two, then toileting becomes simply part of the routine—like washing the face in the morning. It's no longer a major focus of attention and therefore isn't likely to become a battleground for your independent-minded two-year-old.

4) If you start at approximately this age, there's a good chance that your child will be out of diapers by age two and a half. That's a big saving, in money as well as convenience for you.

5) While all young children like to imitate adults, it seems that one-year-olds are especially programmed to imitate. By having your child watch you or older siblings, and supplying her/him with a little potty, you can use that desire to imitate to your advantage. Your one-year-old will probably be delighted to sit on the potty while you're sitting on the toilet.

As with everything else, there are some drawbacks in starting so young. If you're thinking of starting your one-year-old on toilet training, here are a few concerns you should take into account:

1) As with toilet training from birth, the process of training a one-year-old tends to take longer than the process of training a two-year-old. The reason for this is that older

children have a greater capacity for understanding language and direction and may "catch on" faster than younger children.

2) A younger child must be watched with far greater vigilance in the bathroom. While your two-and-a-half-year-old can probably be trusted to take her/himself to the bathroom and use the potty without Mom or Dad's hovering presence, your one-year-old certainly can't do that. (Even your two-year-old will need some supervision, but not as much.) It's dangerous to leave such a young child alone in a bathroom!

3) If you have a child who's very active and won't sit still, you don't have the verbal means yet to communicate to your child *why* you want her/him to sit on the funny chair with the hole in its middle. The child is too young for you to use a trade arrangement ("If you sit on the potty, then I'll take you to the park afterward / give you a cookie / read you a book"). And if s/he happens to slip and fall on the bathroom floor or becomes scared when the toilet flushes, s/he still lacks the verbal and conceptual understanding for you to explain that this wasn't the bathroom or the potty's fault, and there is nothing to be scared of. Your child might develop a long-lasting fear of the potty.

4) At least at the beginning, your one-year-old is a passive recipient of the process (you put her/him on the potty at regular intervals) rather than an active participant. S/he lacks the understanding of *why* you're so excited about the yellow liquid or brown object in the funny white bowl. S/he'll probably be pleased that Mom or Dad is pleased. But s/he might also be a little bewildered. An older child can understand cause and effect, can more easily associate her/his bodily sensations with the objects in the potty. You can more easily explain, using books, videos, drawings, and so on (see Chapter 5, "First Steps"), what the process is

all about and why you're so thrilled with her/his accomplishments.

5) Some two-year-olds are actually *calmer* than one-year-olds! The initial exploratory phase that the new crawler or walker goes through is over. Most two-year-olds are no longer crawling all over the room, minutely examining and tasting every piece of lint and intently inspecting every object. These children have been mobile for close to two years, and are ready to turn their attention to other things.

6) As your child nears age three, s/he may be interested in going to nursery school or play group. This can be a great motivator for her/him to use the potty, because most schools won't accept children who are still in diapers.

Whatever you decide, here are several reasons that should *not* enter into your deliberations.

1) You want your child to be the first on the block to be toilet trained, because you think that means s/he will be smarter, neater, sweeter, more coordinated, or more advanced than other children. Toilet training is not a contest or a competition!

2) Relatives and neighbors shake their fingers at you and tell you that *their* children were trained by the time they were one-year-old, and it's disgraceful how permissive today's parents are.

3) You think changing diapers is a pain in the neck.

4) You think there's something wrong with you if your child is still wearing diapers at age two.

5) You think that the bathroom is the arena for establishing your authority, and the sooner your child learns it, the better.

Whether you start the process when your child is age one or age two, many of the same steps will be taken. For this reason, I have written Chapter 5, "First Steps," so that you can use the suggested techniques whatever age your child is.

REFERENCES

Azrin, Nathan H. and Foxx, Richard M. *Toilet Training in Less than a Day*. Simon and Schuster, 1974.

Fraiberg, Selma. *Every Child's Birthright*. New York: Basic Books, 1977.

Leidloff, Jean. *The Continuum Concept*. New York: Alfred A. Knopf, 1977.

Schaeffer, Charles and DiGeronimo, Theresa Foy. *Toilet Training Without Tears*. New York: Signet Books, 1989.

5

First Steps

This chapter will lead you through the early stages of toilet training. Whether you choose to start when your child is a year old, or whether you decide to wait until s/he's two, these will be useful first steps toward toileting. Read through them to see which are in keeping with your lifestyle and personality, and with your child's age and interests.

TEACH YOUR CHILD ABOUT WET AND DRY

Motivating your child to stay dry requires an ability to understand the concept of wetness and dryness. You can't praise Timmy for having a dry diaper or dry underwear if he has no idea what that means.

You can introduce Timmy to wet and dry by pointing out different things that are wet and dry. When you wash his hands, you can say, "Look, your hands are wet! The water is wet!" You can draw his attention to wet laundry, wet hair, wet grass, and so on. You can have him touch his shirt before putting it on, and say, "Feel that? Your shirt is dry!"

Help your child understand her/his bodily sensations and

51

make the connection between urination and defecation, and the state of her/his diapers by pointing it out. You can tell when Anna is defecating, for example, because she pauses in play and becomes very still. Sometimes she grunts, grimaces, or makes other squeezing noises that alert you to what's going on. Every now and then, during diaper changes or baths, Anna will urinate.

When these things happen, point them out to your child. "Oh, you're making a BM!"(or "Number 2" or "Poop" or whatever term you decide to use). "You just made a wee-wee" (or "pee," or "tinkle," or whatever). When you change your child's diaper afterward, draw her/his attention to the connection between urination or defecation, and the changing of the diaper. "You peed before, and your diaper's wet, so Mommy's changing it. Ah, now your diaper is nice and dry." If you do this regularly, then in time, your child will begin to associate a particular set of bodily sensations with the concepts of "wet" and "dry." This lays the foundation for communicating about toileting.

For a preverbal child, sometimes a sound as well as a word will be helpful. One mother imitated the sound of her child's squeezing noises every time he moved his bowels. The child was fourteen months old and not yet verbal. But several weeks later, when he began to alert her to his need to move his bowels, he used the sound he had learned from his mother.

TALK TO YOUR CHILD ABOUT TOILETING

No matter how old your child is, be clear and verbal in conveying your expectations. When you change a diaper, you might say something like this: "You just made a BM in your diaper. But you know, Mommy and Daddy make our BMs in the toilet. So do your sister and brother and aunts and uncles. One day you'll do that, too." When you're bathing your child, you can point to the toilet and say quite casually, "This is where I pee. One day you'll pee in the toilet, too."

Of course, your child may not fully understand what you're talking about just yet, especially if s/he's preverbal. But explaining things clearly to a child is an excellent habit to develop and begins long before the child is capable of comprehending the actual words. And once s/he can conduct a conversation with you, anything you attempt to teach or do—including toilet training—will proceed more smoothly if there is a communication of your wants to your child.

CHOOSE A POTTY WITH YOUR CHILD

Whatever potty you decide to use (see Chapter 3, "Choosing a Potty"), if you are going to buy a new one, then try to bring your child along with you to choose it. Most children will have some preferences as to style, color, and so on.

Your child will also develop some association between the potty and a fun trip with Mommy or Daddy. By linking the potty with an enjoyable activity, you're building pleasant associations, however subtle they may be. These will have a positive impact on the entire process.

ALLOW YOUR CHILD TO BECOME FAMILIAR WITH THE POTTY

Once you've brought the potty home (or have dusted off the one in the attic that you used for your older children), then allow it to stand in the bathroom for a while, so that your child can get used to it. Let her/him sit on it, open and close it, and become familiar with it for several days before you actually begin to encourage sitting on it. That way it will be a familiar object, and your child is less likely to approach it with consternation or fear.

THE LOCATION OF THE POTTY

The decision about where to put the potty is a very personal one. Some people feel strongly that the bathroom is the only location for bathroom functions and that you might as well start teaching your child so from the beginning.

Other parents feel differently. They put the potty anywhere that's convenient for them—kitchen, bedroom, basement, backyard. This is especially the case when the bathroom is upstairs and there's no bathroom downstairs, or when the bathroom is so busy that the child is likely to go through a lengthy wait before being able to relieve her/himself.

In this, as in other decisions, there is no single right way. Look at your own beliefs and home setup, and decide accordingly. When you do, keep in mind the following factors:

1) Is your bathroom convenient to the rooms that you frequent? If you have to go up two flights of stairs every time your child needs to go (and remember, there can be many "false alarms," especially at the beginning), then you may have lots of extra running to do. What's more, if the child really *does* need to go, then s/he may not be able to hold it in until you get to the bathroom.

2) How old is your child? Small children should *not* be left alone in the bathroom because they can (depending on their age) open the toilet, fall in, and drown (yes, it has happened to several children). They can climb up on the toilet and reach for toothpaste, soap, and other unsafe items in the medicine chest, or slip and fall onto the hard tile floor. Some children might even turn on the bathtub faucets and scald themselves or drown. Bathrooms are notorious places for children to lock themselves in and find themselves unable to open the door. Until a child is able to understand safety, don't leave her/him alone on the potty. It might be better to situate the potty in full view of the room in which you work most often while you go about your business.

There are ways to make your bathroom safer. Toilet safety guards are available in many children's stores. Like cabinet guards, they ensure that the toilet can't be opened by a toddler's curious little fingers. Medicines and other dangerous substances can be put completely out of reach— even climbing reach—or put into a locked cabinet. You can carpet the floor or put down soft bathroom floor mats. Always keep the boiler turned down, so that even the hot faucet won't run scalding water. Remove any locks from the door that can't be opened from the outside by an adult. This will maximize the safety of your bathroom. But even with these precautions, it isn't safe or wise to leave a very young child alone in the bathroom.

Seat Your Child on the Potty at Times of Anticipated Excretion

Many children are regular in their bowel movements, producing them at approximately the same time each day. For some, it's after meals, when the food stimulates the entire digestive tract, leading to the expulsion of stored wastes. For others, it's after a morning nap or before bed. Whatever it may be for your child, try to take note of these patterns. Then seat your child on the potty at the times when you think a bowel movement is likely.

Some children don't seem to have a discernible pattern. That's fine, too. If you've scratched your head in bewilderment about your child's erratic schedule of movements, then stop trying to figure it out. Just seat her/him at regular intervals—say, every hour—on the potty.

Whether your child has regular movements or not, you will still need to seat her/him on the potty at regular intervals so as to catch the release of urine, which rarely follows a predictable pattern.

So just don't expect your child to camp out in the bathroom for hours until a bowel movement comes. Let her/him sit there for a few minutes—even less, if she's antsy. Then if nothing comes out, announce cheerfully, "Oh, well, you didn't make anything this time. That's OK. Maybe next time you'll make a pee or a BM." Bring him back to the potty a short while later to try again. Continue this procedure throughout the day and in the days to follow until he seems able to consistently alert you to his need to make before he has done so.

Congratulations! By now, with hope, you've laid the groundwork for potty training by teaching your child about wet and dry and by helping her/him to become aware of bodily signals and functions. You've devised a communication system to let you know of the need to go. You've taught about the appropriate place to make and what to do afterward. Your child is using the potty—at least some of the time. You're well on your way!

If snags and glitches have appeared at any point along the way, then consult Chapter 9, "General Tips," and Chapter 8, "Toilet Training the Older Child," for further discussion.

TINKLE, TINKLE, LITTLE STAR!

If your child has urinated or has had a BM in the potty, this is cause for applause indeed! Your child is a star! Sure, s/he may not know at first why you're so excited, and may be quite puzzled by your glee. But if you greet each production with enthusiasm, your child will eventually catch on and associate your approval with her/his excretion and will be motivated to repeat the action that elicited your response.

Many parents wonder if they should give a reward to their child for using the potty, such as a cookie, a sticker, or a small toy. This is really a personal decision based on your beliefs about offering material rewards to children for desired behavior. Some parents feel that a tangible reward is an extra incentive for their child and that the heightened motivation will lead to a speedier training process. Others feel that children should learn to obey their parents' wishes without material rewards. Parental approval is in and of itself sufficient reward. They point out as well that some children might continue to ask for the cookie every time they go, long after toileting is a routine and no longer needs to be reinforced each time.

As with so many other decisions, there is no right or wrong way to do it. Examine your own beliefs about rewards, and act accordingly. Think also about your child's reactions. Some children *do* respond more intensely to tangible rewards than to parental approval. But most respond quite well to parental approval, without any additional reward. Most children want to please their parents and are delighted when they accomplish that end.

Parental approval is especially effective when it's communicated with energy and intensity. Children love excitement. That's why they enjoy jack-in-the-box toys, peek-a-boo games, and other activities that involve elements of surprise, motion, and fun. If parents convey their delight in their child's accomplishment with claps, hugs, and an animated face and voice, the message will get through more meaningfully than if they're bland and indifferent.

Toilet training is an excellent area to learn to greet desired behavior enthusiastically, and undesired behavior calmly and blandly. Each time your child makes in the potty or has a dry diaper, celebrate this success! Greet the inevitable "accidents"—whether deliberate or unintentional—with matter-of-fact calm. (See Chapter 7, "The One-Day Intensive Approach" section on Consequences for Wet Pants.)

Even if you are not the type to bubble and enthuse, at least try to convey your pleasure to your child with smiles, hugs, and warm praise. The better your child feels about productions in the potty, the more s/he will try to repeat them.

THE ROYAL FLUSH

Most psychologists advise parents to avoid flushing the toilet while the child is in the room. They offer several reasons for this.

1) Many children find the noise of flushing to be scary. To us, as adults, flushing is such an ordinary and familiar sound that we scarcely pay attention to it. We also have the conceptual ability to understand that the noise is caused by the rush of water in the bowl and is nothing to be afraid of.

Children, on the other hand, are more easily frightened. The noise of a flushing toilet may sound like a tidal wave to them. They also lack the conceptual apparatus to understand how a toilet works and are often impervious to the reassurances of adults that "there is nothing to be afraid of." Psychologists have reported that some children, even as old as five or six years old, still speak of the "toilet monster" who inhabits the bathroom. They posit that children who are exposed to toilet flushing at an early age may

come to see the bathroom as a scary place and avoid it at
all costs.

2) According to many psychologists, very young children can't understand the basic differentiation that human
beings make between "self" and "not-self." They may see
their own waste as part of themselves, although it is no
longer attached to their bodies, and can become scared and
puzzled when their parents push a handle, and part of
"themselves" is whisked away by a rush of water. They
might worry that they, too, will be spirited away by the
water in the porcelain bowl.

3) Some psychologists offer yet a third reason. They
point out that when parents applaud their child's production—for example, a piece of artwork—they save it. They
hang it up on the wall or proudly display it on the mantel-
piece. Now, after the child's bowel movement has been
celebrated and pointed to with pride, it's suddenly disposed
of. This might lead to confusion on the part of the child.

It's certainly true that some children are scared of toilet
noises and cling, terrified, to their parents' legs until the
"storm" is over. It's also true, however, that other children
find the sound to be funny, and the sight of the swirling
water to be fascinating. This is especially the case if your
child is accustomed to being taken into the bathroom while
you, your other children, or child guests are using the toilet.
Or if you just take the child into the room and flush down
toilet paper or tissues as a game, laughing with your child
as you watch the tissue disappear down the drain. Once the
child is ready to have her/his own waste flushed away, it's
no big deal.

Certainly it's wise to be cautious. You lose nothing by
leaving the urine or movement in the potty until you can
quietly flush it away without your child's knowledge. But

this is not written in stone. It is best to allow your child to guide you.

Some children like to wave "bye-bye" to the movement as it disappears. You can cheerfully send it on its way. You might also want to offer some explanation as to where the waste goes when it leaves your bathroom. While you don't need to offer a detailed dissertation on the plumbing system, you might explain in simple terms that the movements travel through pipes under the house and street to special places where they are cleaned up. Or, in even simpler terms—you might say that they've gone "to be with their friends, other pees and BMs."

Sooner or later, of course, you will want to teach your child to flush. We certainly want to teach our children hygiene and consideration for others. As they get older, and more accustomed to the bathroom, it will be time to start introducing flushing as a routine part of toileting.

BATHROOM ROUTINES

Some people don't consider a child to be really toilet trained until s/he can fully go through the entire process of toileting independently—pulling down the pants, sitting on the potty, emptying the potty into the toilet, wiping her/himself, flushing the toilet, and washing their hands. Others say that toilet training has been accomplished when the child is producing most of her/his wastes in the potty or toilet. While it seems foolish to quibble over definitions, it's certainly true that complete independence is the ultimate goal. Sooner or later, the child must learn to carry out the various steps of toileting all by her/himself. The sooner you begin to teach, the better.

So encourage your child to do as much as possible by her/himself. One-year-olds lack the physical control to independently lower their pants, turn on the faucets, and so on. But you can guide their hands through the motions, at least some of the time. Older children can do more on their own. You may have to go over the relevant spots after your child has finished wiping her/himself. But eventually, your child will be self-sufficient in the bathroom.

Some books believe that it should be the child's responsibility to empty the potty her/himself. If your child wants to, that's great! Give her/him every encouragement. But if your child is reluctant or there are many spills, don't worry. There's no need to push her/him to assume responsibility for emptying the potty. After all, the potty is a transitional receptacle. Ultimately your child will be using the toilet, which obviously doesn't need to be ''emptied''—just flushed.

Remember, too, to teach proper wiping techniques to your child. Little girls should always wipe from front to back. This keeps them from introducing fecal material into their vagina, which might result in vaginal infections. Girls should be encouraged to wipe themselves even after urination, because the uric acid, when left upon the skin, might lead to soreness akin to diaper rash.

"I'VE GOT TO GO!"

While the early stages of toilet training often involve ''catching'' the movement or urine in the potty, which is a feat of second guessing and opportune timing, you don't want to do that forever. You want your child to be aware of the need to go, motivated to go in the potty, and able to signal the need to go so that you can escort her/him.

Even if your child is already aware of the sensations that accompany excretion, and is also eager to carry out these activities in the potty, s/he may not yet be in tune with the need to go *before* it happens. So you may find at the beginning, that the child signals *after* the movement has already started. See this as a positive sign! It's simply a transitional step. S/he will soon come to recognize the need to go before the process has started.

Remember—try not to react to the discovery of urine or bowel movement in your child's diaper with disappointment or disapproval.

WORK AS A TEAM

It is important for couples to share toilet training responsibilities. If only one person is involved—let's say only Mom is taking Karen to the bathroom—then Karen might be reluctant to use the potty with Dad. But if Mom and Dad alternate, Karen becomes used to both and is equally comfortable whether it's Mom or Dad who's escorting her to the bathroom. The same applies to older siblings, grandparents, or baby-sitters.

Make sure you coordinate your terminology and approach with all the people involved in training your child. If your child expects reminders, for instance, be sure everyone responsible for caring for her/him knows this. If you're telling Joey that the only place for urination is the bathroom, make sure Dad isn't setting up little cups for him to aim into in the kitchen. If you allow Nancy to play with her favorite dolly while she's on the potty, make sure Mom is aware of this, too.

Try as well to coordinate your terminology. Consistency is reassuring and reduces confusion. If you're talking about "BMs" and "wee-wees," while Grandpa talks about "Number One" and "Number Two," and the babysitter talks about "poop" and "pee," your child might end up feeling pretty confused. The same applies to the words you use to describe bodily parts. Most families prefer euphemisms—just make sure that once you've decided on a term, you stick to it, at least at the beginning.

OTHER HELPFUL AIDES/IDEAS

Pottying by the Book

Some children love to read. Even if they can't talk or understand words yet, they love to cuddle up with their parents and look at pictures. For these children, there are many wonderful books on the market that are designed to introduce children to the potty. *Once Upon a Potty* by Alona Frankel is a classic. (She has written two different versions, by the way—one for boys and one for girls.) *Toilet Learning: The Picture Book Technique for Children and Parents* by Alison Mack is also excellent. Fred Rogers of *Mister Rogers' Neighborhood* has written a book called *Going to the Potty,* and Anna Ross has written a book called *I Have to Go,* which uses Sesame Street characters. These are just a few of the books on the market aimed at a toddler/preschooler audience.

Reading to children is a wonderful way to become closer to them. And seeing something written in a book often makes a deep impression on them and reinforces what parents are trying to teach. In the case of toileting, seeing a character in a book learn about using the potty will help familiarize your child with what's expected and may inspire imitation.

If your child is the bouncy, frisky type who won't sit still long enough to read, or if s/he likes to chew on books instead of looking at the contents, then there are other techniques available.

Videos

Some children don't want to sit still and read a book but are riveted to a television screen. There are several videos available, including *Once Upon a Potty* by Alona Frankel. It would be best if you could sit down with your child and watch and make comments (just as you would if you were reading to her/him), at least the first time the video is viewed.

Other Useful Toys

There are children who don't like reading or television. That's OK—there are plenty of other toys that will encourage them in the direction of toileting.

Drawing together is fun and can be used to pursue the goal of toilet training. You can tell a story using crayons or markers, draw a toilet with someone sitting on it—indeed anything you want that will introduce the toilet and its purpose to your child. Some children are interested in seeing a picture of a familiar object develop right before their eyes, as the adult draws a bathroom and shows little "people" going in to use the toilet. It might be fun and interesting, too, to ask your child to draw you a picture of the bathroom, its equipment, and functions.

Clay or Play-Doh can be used in a similar manner, to shape the familiar bathroom equipment—sink, toilet, bathtub, or shower stall—and people using the equipment appropriately. You can explain as you go along.

Make sure you don't turn these drawing or clay sessions into dull lessons or drudgery. Leave plenty of time for your child to do free play with the crayons and clay. After all, you don't want your child to feel resentful, bored, or pushed too hard.

These ideas are obviously not appropriate for a child who doesn't understand the function of crayons or clay—who chews them or stuffs them into her/his nostrils, for example. Some children—even some one-year-olds—are ready to use drawing equipment or Play-Doh. They understand the function of the various objects and use them correctly. Others don't. Use your own judgment where your child is concerned.

Role Models

Children learn best from watching others and imitating them. That's how they learn to speak, write, use cutlery, and a host of other important skills. Sometimes, this can be quite funny. Sally is talking to her dolls, and suddenly you hear an uncanny imitation of yourself. You watch her swagger out the door with a briefcase, and laugh as you see a reflection of yourself going off to the office.

Children are usually as eager to copy toileting practices as they are to copy everything else. So the more you can arrange for your child to observe others in the bathroom, the better. If s/he has older siblings, then involve them in your plan! Some siblings will have no objection to showing their younger sibs what to do, and might even feel proud of their role as mentor and guide. If this is the case, then start by having your toddler—whether age one or two—observe older sisters or brothers on a regular basis. Then suggest that she/he sit on the potty while the older sibling sits on the toilet. Most children love having "little" versions of grown-up items (such as telephones, brooms, desks, cutlery) and using them while the adults use theirs, and will probably be charmed by their pint-sized toilet.

It would be best if male children could observe older brothers, while female children observe older sisters. That's not essential however. Both sexes sit when they move their bowels. If a female child is watching an older boy urinate, it would be better for him to sit down so as to model the behavior that you want your daughter to imitate.

Some little boys stand up to urinate right away; others start by sitting down. There is no need for an older brother to alter his style and sit down for the sake of his younger brother.

If there are no siblings, or if the siblings are reluctant to become involved, then try to find different contexts for your child to watch others in the bathroom. Bring your child into the bathroom with you, if you are comfortable with this idea. When you are away from home you can go into public bathrooms where your child will observe other adults using the restroom. You can visit a nursery school bathroom, if the school is amenable, and your child can watch other children engaged in bathrooming. The more you do this, the more your child will get the message that this is a normal, everyday activity that everyone does, and the more s/he will be inspired to follow suit.

Bring Your Child to Many Bathrooms

Whether your child is ready to use the bathroom or not, try to visit as many bathrooms as possible together. Again, this will communicate the idea that bathrooms are every-where—in the library, the department store, at Grandma's house, in the restaurant.

Using a Wetting Doll

While children learn the most from human role models, using a doll that wets can be a helpful device as well. This is emphasized as a central feature in Chapter 7, One-Day Intensive Approach of Foxx and Azrin. But even if you're not using this particular approach, the wetting doll is still useful. Most children love feeding the bottle to the doll and watching it "pee" afterward. You can place the doll on a potty, or better—show your child how to tend to the doll her/himself. Remember to praise the doll, as you would praise your child for making in the potty.

There are dolls available that produce bowel movements, not just "urine." They tend to be rather expensive—but if you decide to buy one, it'll be useful to teach your child about making bowel movements as well as urine in the potty. It's nice, but certainly not necessary.

REFERENCES AND SUGGESTED READING

Frankel, Alona. *Once Upon a Potty*. Woodbury, NY: Barron's Educational Series, 1990.

Lansky, Vicki. *Koko Bear's New Potty*. New York: Bantam Books, 1986.

Mack, Alison. *Toilet Learning: The Picture Book Technique for Children and Parents*. Little, Brown Inc., 1978.

Rogers, Fred. *Going to the Potty*. New York: Putnam, 1986.

Ross, Anna. *I Have to Go*. New York: Random House Children's Television Workshop, 1990.

6

Good-bye Diapers! Welcome Training Pants!

If your child is using the potty most of the time, then you've reached an important milestone. Your child is ready for training pants!

WHAT ARE TRAINING PANTS?

Training pants are underwear specially designed for the child who's in the process of being trained. Usually they are thicker, therefore more absorbent than ordinary underpants, in case the child accidentally wets or soils.

WHAT KINDS OF TRAINING PANTS ARE AVAILABLE?

There are several different kinds of training pants on the market. Some are made of thick, extra-absorbent cloth or terry cloth. Others have an outer plastic shell covering the cloth. Some companies are now manufacturing disposable training pants.

At the beginning, when accidents can be frequent, it helps to have training pants with a plastic shell. Cloth training pants are somewhat more absorbent than ordinary single-layer underwear—which is ideal for a child who's more advanced and can "catch" her/himself as the urine or movement begins to come out, signal, and be taken to the bathroom quickly. But for children who do not yet have such a high degree of awareness and control, cloth training pants by themselves do little to prevent a river from running down the child's leg (and onto the carpet or furniture) in case of an accident. The plastic helps contain the liquid, as well as any solid that might have been produced.

My experience has been that some of the training pants that come with attached plastic shells do not hold out very well in the laundry. The hot water used to disinfect the soiled or wet underwear takes a toll on the plastic. It might be better to buy cloth training pants and a separate plastic shell to put over them. That way each can be washed separately. Plus, once your child has advanced beyond the early stages, you can put away the plastic liners, reserving them perhaps for long trips in the car or other situations in which you're concerned about whether your child can "hold it" until s/he gets to the bathroom. You'll be left with a stack of usable cloth training pants, which your child will probably wear for quite a while.

Disposable training pants are now available in supermarkets. They are similar to diapers but are shaped like underpants. They also don't have a plastic covering. They, too, are excellent for making the transition between diapers and training pants. They save lots of washing and scrubbing (and often leakage as well) if your child wets or soils. They're also wonderful for traveling, when carting around wet or dirty underwear might be inconvenient.

There are several disadvantages, however, to the disposable training pants. One is that they *feel* like diapers, and some children don't get the message that they're wearing training pants. The second problem is that they're rather expensive. The third is that using disposables always takes a toll on the environment. All these factors must be taken into consideration when you're making the decision about which training pants to buy.

LET YOUR CHILD HELP YOU CHOOSE

When you're ready to choose training pants, try to bring your child along. This serves the same purpose as it did when you brought her/him along to choose a potty. Your child feels involved. S/he's justifiably proud, and a trip with Mom or Dad is a wonderful way to cheer her/him along. Your child may have preferences for a particular design and will more eagerly wear the underpants if you honor those tastes.

CHOOSE INTERESTING DESIGNS

Many children love to wear clothing with attractive pictures and designs. Whether you're shopping on your own or taking your child with you, try to choose training pants that will look appealing to her/his eyes. If your child has some strong interest—for example, in cars and trucks, or in the ABC—you might look for pants with those designs. Many children love to see their television "friends" on their clothing, and will be delighted to wear Big Bird or Ninja Turtle underwear.

MAKE SURE THEY FIT

It's important to be sure that the training pants you choose are the appropriate size for your child. Pants that are too large will keep falling down. Even if they don't drop to the floor, it's a nuisance for you or your child to keep having to hitch them up. Pants that are too small will feel uncomfortable and tight and will also be difficult for your child to lower without help.

TALK TO YOUR CHILD

When you give your child the new training pants, use a little fanfare! After all, Bobby is graduating from "baby" diapers to "big-boy" underwear! Help him feel proud. At the same time, be aware that some children are reluctant to relinquish their babyhood. There are certain advantages in being a baby, and your child might be a little afraid of the new responsibilities that being more "grown-up" might entail. So if Maureen seems a little uneasy about this new step, take the time to talk to her. Reassure her of your ongoing love. Explain that becoming a "big girl" doesn't mean giving up cuddling, playing with dolls, or whatever else she likes to do. Try as well to emphasize the advantages of being more grown-up—special privileges, trips, or other activities from which she has been excluded as a result of being too young.

Some children feel that the introduction of training pants creates a pressure situation in which they *must* make in the potty all the time and *never* have an accident. They feel they must become perfect overnight.

Reassure your child that this isn't the case. While, of course, you would like her/him to use the potty, no one expects perfection—just the very best possible effort. Your love remains equally strong, no matter what.

NIGHTTIME DRYNESS

Most children remain wet at night long after they achieve daytime control. There are those few children who achieve nighttime control before they are fully dry by day. This is unusual and seems to happen in a case where the child is busy and involved with play during the day and therefore unwilling to take the time to respond to Nature's call. In other words, the child is completely aware of her/his bodily signals at night and by day, but allows other activities to take priority during the day.

Most children, however, are not so supremely aware of a full bladder during the night. It takes time to learn your body's language, especially when you're sleeping. Many children remain in diapers for more than a year after they're trained during the day.

You can begin to put your child in training pants at night when you notice a dry diaper upon waking up for several mornings. Continue to praise your child for waking up dry, even though it's not within conscious control. Nighttime dryness *is* a milestone. Don't get rattled by an occasional accident either. That's normal. Help your child get cleaned up, reassure her/him that you're still proud, and that occasional nighttime accidents are normal.

If your child has been dry for several nights, is already in training pants at night, and suddenly starts to wet again, then ask yourself if s/he's drinking too much right before bed. It might help to limit bedtime fluids to, say, half a cup. Make sure, too, that s/he is urinating immediately before going to sleep. If these don't help, then perhaps your child is still a little too young to stay dry at night. Switch back to diapers, and try again in a few weeks.

If you need to switch back to diapers, be sure to explain to your child why you're doing this. Again, be matter-of-fact, calm, and reassuring. Explain that many children have trouble staying dry at night at the beginning, and that you're going to help by allowing nighttime diapers until s/he's a little older. Be sure that you communicate no shame or blame. A young child's bladder capacity is still small. Sammy may be unable to hold in his urine for as long a period of time as a whole night. As he grows, his bladder will grow with him.

If your child has been trained for a while and is still unable to remain dry at night, then read Chapter 10, "Defining and Preventing Bed-wetting."

When your child begins to sleep in training pants, you might want to buy a rubber-lined sheet to use in the crib or bed. If this is too hot for your child, then put a regular sheet over it. That way, if an accident takes place, the mattress won't get ruined.

CLOTHING IN GENERAL

It's even more important now to provide easy-to-handle clothing for your child. Now that Barbara's wearing underwear, she will start to grow in independence, learning more and more to take herself to the bathroom instead of calling for your assistance. So clothes that are difficult for small fingers to manipulate—clothes with a multiplicity of complex buttons, snaps, or ties, and clothes that close at the back—should definitely be avoided. Even clothes that can be managed by your child but which will take a very long time—like overalls, which hook up over the shoulders—will add unnecessary complications to toileting. Young children often are so busy with play that they wait until "the last minute" to respond to Nature's calls. Those extra moments of fiddling with overalls instead of simply lowering a pair of pants may mean the difference between wet and dry clothing. Some children find overalls and other such clothes difficult and may hold back going to the bathroom until it's too late, rather than face the potentially frustrating task of undressing themselves.

Since it's likely that there will be at least a few accidents, no matter how easy you've made it for your child to undress her/himself, be prepared: Try to dress your child in clothes that you don't care about for the first few weeks. That way if s/he wets or soils, you won't be concerned about stains that might not wash out perfectly. Plastic shoes or sandals will wipe clean more easily than canvas or leather. Doing this won't just protect your child's clothes. It'll protect *you* from that exclamation of anger or disappointment. It'll be easier to remain calm, matter-of-fact, and neutral if you don't care so much about the clothes your child is wearing.

PROTECTING YOUR FURNITURE

Just like you'll want to protect your child's best clothing from the wetting or soiling that is likely to occur during those first weeks in training pants, so, too, will you want to protect your furniture and carpets. So as often as possible, try to keep your child in rooms with furniture and flooring that is easy to clean—the kitchen, the den, the bathroom. If you live in a small apartment or some other situation in which this is impossible, then you might want to cover your couch or armchair with plastic, and even consider keeping a plastic drop cloth over your floor. Don't worry about how it looks. After all, it's only for a few weeks, until your child is further along the toilet training journey.

Remember—plastic bags can be very dangerous for children! If you *do* decide to cover your floor or furniture with plastic, make sure your child is fully supervised at all times! It takes only a few moments for a child to suffer from lack of oxygen and die.

There are two alternatives to plastic covering: rubber-backed sheets (which you may decide to use in your child's bed or crib when s/he starts to wear training pants at night); and thick toweling. While terry cloth towels won't protect your couch with the same foolproof dryness as plastic, they do provide some protection and are very useful. If you lead a very busy life and will be unable to provide the scrupulous supervision required if you're using plastic, then a layer or two of towels might be your best bet.

If your child does wet or soil your furniture or carpet, then here's how to clean it so that it comes out as free of odor and staining as possible:

(1) Wipe away any solid waste.

(2) Use a dry cloth to absorb all excess liquid.

(3) Wet a cloth with water, and douse the area.

(4) Follow any laundering instructions that might come with your furniture or carpet.

(5) Absorb as much water as possible with dry cloth.

(6) For faster drying, turn on the fan and point it toward the wet area.

(7) Sprinkle with baking soda to absorb any remaining odors.

(8) Allow baking soda to remain for a while, then vacuum.

7

The One-Day Intensive Approach

The one-day intensive approach was developed by Drs. Nathan H. Azrin and Richard M. Foxx and is detailed in their book *Toilet Training in Less than a Day*. Their initial efforts at developing a toilet training program were aimed at the profoundly retarded population, many of whom had hitherto been considered untrainable. When they realized how successful their program had been with people of impaired intelligence, they reasoned that it could be modified and adapted to children with whom retardation was not a problem.

Their stated goal is to "teach your child to toilet himself with the same independence as an adult, and without the need for reminders, continued praise or assistance" (page 39). In order to do so, there are a list of skills that they want the child to learn:

1) Seating her/himself on the potty chair
2) Raising and lowering the underpants alone
3) Relaxing and releasing the urine into the potty
4) Wiping
5) Emptying the potty
6) Flushing the toilet

7) Learning to be entirely self-motivated throughout the process, to recognize and respond to bodily signals without parental guidance, reminders, or praise

Quite a tall order! But the authors present a systematic set of steps to achieve these goals.

BE SURE YOUR CHILD IS READY

Foxx and Azrin feel that a child under twenty months old is probably not ready for their approach. Even some twenty-month-olds may not yet be ready. In order to determine your child's readiness, they suggest that you ask yourself certain questions:

1) Is your child dry for significant stretches of time (a few hours)? Does s/he seem aware ahead of time of being about to urinate? Is there a significant quantity of urine when urination does occur? (Even if s/he's not aware ahead of time, don't worry. Not all children do this and they may still be ready for this approach.)

2) Is your child developed physically? Can s/he pick up objects? Walk independently?

3) Does s/he have receptive language? Can s/he point to different parts of her/his body? Can s/he follow simple instructions? Foxx and Azrin suggest an "Instructional Readiness Test," a series of questions to ask to determine your child's ability to be verbally instructed.

If you have answered yes to the above questions, then your child is ready. If not, wait a few weeks, then reassess the situation.

LAYING THE GROUNDWORK

Foxx and Azrin feel that you can set the stage for their approach well in advance, even while your child is very young, by allowing her/him to dress her/himself as much as possible; watch others using the toilet; teach her/him key terminology such as "wet" and "dry" and the words you will use for urine and feces; do not allow tantrums to sway you when you give your child an instruction to carry out. This way your tantrum policy will be old hat to your child if and when s/he decides to throw a tantrum during the training.

SETTING THE STAGE

1) Foxx and Azrin suggest the kitchen as the best location to train your child.

2) They suggest stocking sweet drinks and food treats, both salty and sweet.

3) They recommend buying a potty to place in the kitchen, and they discuss the pros and cons of various potties. The most important feature is that the potty's bowl should be easily detachable by your child, who will be taught to empty it her/himself.

4) Aside from the potty, you will need to buy a wetting doll, which will be used to demonstrate to your child the desired behavior (see Chapter 5, "First Steps").

5) Try to review in your mind the significant personalities (real or fictional) in your child's life. Make a list. They will be the "Friends Who Care"—those people who you will tell your child are pleased with successful pottying or displeased with accidental wetting.

6) Eliminate distractions—radios, televisions, toys, cooking, and so on. Have siblings cared for by others, keep your phone on an answering machine, and deal with unexpected callers quickly, returning at once to your child.

7) Buy several pairs of loose-fitting cloth training pants.

8) Coordinate training with other adults in the house so that they are also involved. Be sure that you are focused on the training rather than each other.

9) Make sure your child has had a good night's sleep and is in good health.

USING THE WETTING DOLL

The first step in the training is teaching your child to assist a wetting doll in pottying. Your child will be teaching the doll in the same way that you will be teaching your child.

GIVE YOUR CHILD PLENTY TO DRINK

The tremendous quantity of drinking serves two purposes: A sweet drink can serve as a reward for dry pants; and the drinking increases the volume of liquid in the bladder, creating a more frequent need to urinate. The more your child practices urinating in the potty, the more the behavior will become an established part of her/his personality.

TEACH YOUR CHILD TO SIT ON THE POTTY

You will be keeping a written record of "potty trials," which will occur every 15 minutes. Eventually, your child will figure out that s/he is expected to urinate there. You will praise her/him, demonstrate proper wiping, and show how the potty is emptied.

At first, your child will need reminders to use the potty. But Foxx and Azrin suggest a procedure that will gradually phase out the need for reminders.

REWARDS

Foxx and Azrin recommend five types of rewards: verbal praise; snack treats; special drinks; citing the "friends who care" list; and nonverbal praise (hugging, stroking, smiling, applauding). Generally speaking, these rewards are to be administered not only when the child urinates in the potty, but when you check the underpants and find them dry.

CONSEQUENCES FOR WET PANTS

When your child has an accident, then several consequences are suggested:

1) "Verbal disapproval"—telling your child that you're disappointed s/he wet her/his pants.
2) "Positive practice"—have your child go through the motions of toileting (going to the potty, lowering the pants, sitting on the potty, and so on) 10 times from various points of the house.
3) "Wet pants awareness"—making the child aware of her/his wet pants and its accompanying sensations.
4) "Cleanliness responsibility"—having your child clean up the puddle s/he made on the floor; remove the wet clothes by her/himself; carry the wet clothes to the hamper; and put on fresh clothes.

WHEN IS MY CHILD CONSIDERED "TRAINED"?

Foxx and Azrin feel that a child has been trained "when he walks to the potty chair for the first time without a reminder and completes the entire toileting experience without the need for instructions or guidance" (page 107). Nevertheless, they suggest continued observation throughout the day. After three additional successfully completed toileting trips, begin to phase out the approval and praise. Pants inspections should continue, but with decreasing frequency. The child can now resume normal activities, but fluid intake should remain high, so as to ensure that s/he continues to need the bathroom frequently. This will teach her/him how to interrupt an interesting game or TV program when s/he needs to urinate.

FOLLOW-UP

According to Foxx and Azrin, most children should be completely trained in less than a day. If your child takes longer, then simply begin the next day by picking up where you left off.

Even a trained child needs follow-up, especially during the first few days after training. Foxx and Azrin suggest:

1) Regular dry-pants inspections.

2) Verbal reprimands if there is an accident.

3) Toileting practice and clean-up after an accident.

4) After one accident-free week, scheduled pants inspections can be terminated.

5) A diploma is to be awarded at the end of the process.

6) Do not revert back to diapers by day, even if there are frequent accidents. If your child has diarrhea, put a plastic liner over the training pants. At night, keep your child in diapers only if s/he is under age two-and-a-half. A child who is older should sleep in training pants, with a rubber or plastic sheet to protect the mattress. (They feel that diapers are too cumbersome and difficult for the child to remove if s/he needs the toilet during the night.)

ADVANTAGES AND DISADVANTAGES OF THIS APPROACH

There are several notable advantages in the less-than-a-day approach.

1) If you and your spouse work full-time, this approach might be excellent for you. Your time is severely limited, and you are not with your child enough on a day-to-day basis to be able to provide the consistent, regular daily involvement necessary to teach your child toileting skills. After all, most of the other approaches in this book recommend taking your child to the potty several times a day over a period of several weeks or months. Obviously this is impossible if you're not home to do it.

Some baby-sitters and day-care centers are willing to work with parents in toilet training. Many, however, are not. They would rather have a child in diapers than deal with the task of toilet training. If you're out of the house most of the time, and your child-care provider is unwilling to toilet train your child, then this is an approach you can use in a single day. You can put aside a Saturday or Sunday (Saturday is better because in case your child doesn't get the hang of it in one day, you can finish up the job on Sunday). The entire day can be devoted to toilet training, with the assurance of the authors that by Monday, your child is almost certain to be trained.

2) If the training is successful, then it's nice to be done with the process in just a day. Although toilet training ideally should be something that draws parents and children closer together, it is often the stage for power struggles and conflicts. For some children, the novelty of the activity, the many snacks and treats, and the realization that they'll have to clean up after themselves from now on if they wet their underwear provide powerful motivation to cooperate. Many months of conflict and friction might be avoided.

3) This approach certainly cuts back on the money and time spent on keeping a child in diapers for a long training period.

4) Some parents (especially working parents) are thrilled by the opportunity to spend a day entirely focused on their child. They are delighted for an excuse to disconnect the phone, suspend all other obligations and activities, and create a sort of bubble in space and time that is occupied solely by them and their child.

5) When the child has been trained using this approach, s/he will be using the potty without adult supervision, reminders, continued rewards, and praise.

6) This approach has an internal consistency, logic, and a step-by-step methodology that is easy to understand and follow. Children usually respond well to a sense of self-confidence in an adult who is clear about her/his intentions and methods.

7) Because this approach incorporates many different modalities—imitation, positive praise and reward, consequences for accidents, and so on—it tends to hasten the learning process.

There have been, however, many questions raised about the less-than-a-day approach.

1) The authors focus exclusively on bladder training and don't deal with bowel training at all. They themselves admit that the training process often happens so fast that the child might not have had a bowel movement during that time. But they feel that "once you have trained your child to urinate properly, he should have no problem with his bowel movements" (page 115). They suggest treating a soiling accident exactly like you would treat a wetting accident.

It may indeed be true: Many children figure out that bowel movements as well as urine are to be deposited in the potty. But some don't deduce that. What's more, the independence that your child can demonstrate in self-toileting (dumping out the urine, wiping her/himself) may be considerably more complicated and less effective when it comes to cleaning and disposing of bowel movements. Children of twenty months really can't do an adequate job wiping themselves, which can lead to soreness in the anal area.

2) Some children adapt well to dramatic and sudden changes. Others, however, seem to do better with more gradual changes. This program, by definition, is advocating a major change in the child's life, which is to occur within a matter of hours. For some children, this may be too abrupt.

3) The single-minded focus on toilet training might be too intense for many parents—and many children.

Children—especially toddlers—are wonderfully curious. They are captivated by so many things. This is part of the wonder of their age. Foxx and Azrin say that when your child introduces an extraneous topic, you should "not allow these comments to distract him and you from the training. Instead, redirect his comment by a statement about the importance of his learning to toilet himself." But if your child senses that you're trying to draw her/him away from an object or topic of great interest, it becomes even more fascinating (the old "forbidden fruits are sweetest" principle). The more you try to redirect her/his attention to toileting, the more fascinating that tree outside the window, or that pattern on the kitchen floor will become. Redirecting your child's attention must be done lovingly and skillfully—a real challenge.

Aside from any psychological difficulty that some parents might experience in arranging a totally distraction-free, all-consuming day devoted to toilet training, there may arise some logistical and practical difficulties as well. If there are younger siblings, it may require some fancy footwork to arrange a full day of child care for them. Pets, too, are not so easily put out of the way for such a long stretch of time. If you have a large household, with many family members on different schedules, it may be difficult to arrange a day in which everyone avoids the kitchen for many hours. (And if older siblings are playing the TV or radio upstairs, are entertaining friends in the basement, or doing their homework in the living room, there's a fair chance that your child will be more interested in all these goings-on than in the potty.) If you decide to do this during the summer or spring, your child may be hankering after the Great Outdoors and may resent being cooped in for so many hours. Planning out a distraction-free day that centers around the kitchen will require a lot of commitment to this approach.

4) Children who have difficulty accepting authority (Foxx and Azrin call them "stubborn" children) will probably do better with other approaches.

5) The authors advise ignoring tantrums and proceeding with the program. But if your child is having a tantrum about toilet training, then it is becoming a battleground rather than a joint cooperative venture. And besides, you can't *force* someone to empty her/his bladder. If your child is crying, kicking, or screaming on the floor, then it's unrealistic to sail blithely along as if the tantrum isn't occurring, or to make sure that your "instruction is carried out"—especially if the instruction involves a body function.

If your child is having tantrums during this program, maybe it's a sign that s/he is experiencing too much pressure regarding toileting. It's probably time to put aside the program, give the whole thing a break, and gently introduce toilet training in a more gradual fashion later on.

6) Many parents take exception to the heavy use of rewards, from an educational as well as a nutritional point of view. They feel that material rewards are neither necessary nor desirable in trying to teach a child (see Chapter 5, ''First Steps''). Additionally, the reliance on ''junk'' snacks to reinforce toileting and to create further need to urinate is nutritionally unsound.

7) The authors recommend ''verbal disapproval'' when a child has wet her/his pants. While they warn parents against anger, yelling, screaming, and against physical punishment, they do suggest statements like ''Wetting is bad'' or ''Only babies like wet pants'' (page 98). They point out that for most children, ''simple verbal disapproval may be sufficient. Other children may require more emphatic disapproval, but spanking or other physical punishment is *probably* [italics mine] never justified'' (pages 98 and 99).

It seems that the authors are opening up a door to parental judgmentalism. I see no reason for a child to *ever* be spanked or scolded for wetting her/his pants. Certainly it is important for your child to realize that you are displeased by an accident. But there is no reason to call wetting ''bad'' or to imply that s/he is like a baby. These comments might take a toll on your child's self-esteem.

8) The authors advise telling your child ''how unhappy you and his heroes are that his pants are wet'' (page 102). There is no reason to become unhappy when your child has had an accident, nor do you wish to convey to your child the message that s/he has power over your happiness and unhappiness. (See Chapter 1, ''Attitude''.)

9) While it's important for children to learn how to assume responsibility for cleaning up after themselves, it's important to guard against making that a ''punishment,'' rather a natural consequence that emanates from a non-angry, loving, accepting internal stance on your part. The authors see the clean-up as a natural consequence rather than a penalty, but other reputable books about toilet training refer to this aspect of the program as a "penalty."

10) The authors seem to go a bit overboard when they recommend 10 practice trips to the potty from different points in the house after each accident. For some children, this may be too tedious, and they may rebel against the entire process.

11) Requiring the child to empty the potty places additional and unnecessary pressure upon the child (especially if you're training her/him in the kitchen). It's a delicate balancing act to carry a bowl of liquid from one room to another without a spill and neatly empty it into the toilet. (See Chapter 5, "First Steps" for a discussion of whether the child should be expected to empty the potty her/himself.)

12) Withdrawing statements and gestures of approval on successful toileting after only one day seems to deprive the child of potential sources of cheering and parental praise. It seems abrupt and unfair. Why *shouldn't* your child continue for several weeks to be praised for her/his new achievement? Praise can be gradually tapered off as the novelty of toileting wears off and you find new achievements and new areas to praise.

13) As discussed in Chapter 5, "First Steps," some children are frightened of the flushing noise of the toilet. Insisting that a child flush the toilet might be insensitive to her/his concerns about the noise of flushing.

14) Some parents are reluctant to use the kitchen for bathroom functions, or the bathroom for eating. (See Chapter 5, "First Steps" for a discussion of the location of the potty.) It's okay to use the bathroom—but Foxx and Azrin seem to imply that you should ideally confine the process to a single room so as to minimize distractions. It might be difficult, not to mention unfair, to try to confine your child to the bathroom for such a long period of time.

15) The authors seem to equate happiness with dryness. Do you really want to teach your child that something as important as inner peace, equanimity, and sense of happiness are dependent upon the state of her/his underwear?

16) The authors suggest putting your child in training pants for the night if s/he is over age two and a half. But studies have shown that a large number of children continue to wet during the night for many months to many years after being dry during the day. Expecting two-and-a-half-year-olds to remain dry at night may be setting them up for frustration and disappointment. (See Chapter 10, ''Defining and Preventing Bed-wetting'' for a more complete discussion of nighttime wetting.)

If after reading the pros and cons you decide that your schedule or personality will be well suited to the one-day approach, then adapt the program accordingly. Remember that *you* are the one training your child. Any book's recommendations, however sensible or creative, can be changed, adapted, or discarded based on your own understanding of yourself, your child, and your life-style. You might try to combine some of the early pretraining readiness steps discussed in Chapter 5 with the one-day approach, thereby really setting the stage so that your child is primed and excited about training. Trust yourself and your child, and allow the process to flow smoothly and easily, without tension, concern about whether you're ''doing it right,'' or pressure on your child.

OTHER ONE-DAY APPROACHES

Some parents report success in training their children in one day even without Foxx and Azrin's program. These seem to be the basic components of their success:

1) The child needs to be close to three and verbal.

2) Discuss in a comfortable, loving, and enthusiastic way that soon Johnny will be ready to learn how to use the toilet "like a big boy." Express your confidence in his ability, the pride you already feel in his accomplishments, and the pride you'll feel when he is trained.

3) If your child balks at the prospect, drop it and bring it up again in a few weeks.

4) Choose a day when you'll do the training. Don't choose a day that will conflict with play group or story time at the library if these are favorite activities. Don't choose a day in which you'll be pressured, tired, or pre-occupied with other things. (You don't need total, single-minded concentration, however.) Make sure your child is healthy and well-rested.

5) Give your child advance notice so that s/he is an active participant in every stage of the process.

6) Remind your child the day before that "tomorrow will be the big day."

7) When you discuss training with Susie, if she seems persistently reluctant, then choose a reward that she will get upon successful completion of the process. Involve her in this choice. While any reward that will be meaningful to the child will do, ideally it should be something that he has been "too young" for until now. Perhaps a trip to the ball game with her/his big brother, or a bike with training wheels in place of the tricycle. My sister trained one little boy by promising him tzitzis—a garment worn by Ortho-dox Jews. It is the custom that untrained children don't wear this garment, because of the concern that the garment may become soiled by contact with a dirty diaper. The tzitzis were bought and formed an incentive for the training. They were presented to him when he had learned to use the potty.

8) Go together to choose the potty and training pants.

Choose interesting designs for the pants.

9) Remove the diapers, and organize the pants in your child's drawer—preferably in a low drawer that will be easily accessible.

10) Take her/him to the potty and wait for urination or defecation to occur. Applaud any production.

11) Set up a toileting schedule and continue to give reminders without nagging. Encourage your child to initiate her/his own toileting.

12) Keep the nighttime diapers, especially at the beginning.

13) Present your child with the reward with a flourish! Continue to praise her/him for several weeks to come, gradually phasing out the praise and moving on to other things.

14) Make sure your attitude remains relaxed, loving, nurturing, and supportive.

If you and your child have an easy, loving relationship, and if your child is enthusiastic and motivated, s/he will probably be trained in a day. And even if it takes longer, it's unlikely to become a protracted process of many months.

REFERENCES

Azrin, Nathan A. and Foxx, Richard M. *Toilet Training in Less Than a Day*. New York: Simon and Schuster, 1974.

Schaeffer, Charles E. and DiGeronimo, Theresa Foy. *Toilet Training Without Tears*. New York: Signet Books, 1989.

8

Toilet Training the Older Child

An "older child" is a child above the age of three and a half who is still not toilet trained. There are several reasons why a child might get into that situation.

MEDICAL PROBLEMS

There are a number of physiological problems that may interfere with toilet training. Many of them have been dealt with in other chapters (see Chapter 9, "General Tips," and Chapter 11, "Encopresis"). If you've been trying to train your child but to no avail, start by consulting your pediatrician. S/he will rule out urinary or bowel diseases and will advise you how to treat them if they're present.

Depending on the nature and severity of the problem, your doctor may request further testing, diagnostic procedures, or even surgery. (See Chapter 11, "Encopresis" for a longer discussion of how to prepare your child for the experience of undergoing a series of medical procedures that may be invasive or painful.)

THE CHILD WHO'S NEVER BEEN TAUGHT

Could it be possible that you simply never took your child's training in hand? Perhaps you believed that it wasn't your place to teach your child to use the potty, and that one day s/he would teach her/himself. Perhaps you just never got around to it. Don't worry. It's never too late.

Your best bet would be to follow the steps outlined in Chapter 7 (the section called "Other One-Day Approaches"). This program is most effective with healthy children who are over age three and haven't been trained yet. You might need to include some sensory training—helping your child become aware of wet and dry underwear. (Many children who've grown up in today's highly sophisticated extra-absorbent diapers never develop the awareness that they're wet.) If you approach your child with a sense of confidence in yourself, confidence in your child, love and warmth, then your child should catch on pretty quickly.

THE RESISTANT CHILD

Some children seem to have learned from the old nursery rhyme "Mary, Mary, quite contrary." Whatever you want them to do, they will predictably go ahead and do the opposite. You ask them to eat their oatmeal, and they'll tip the bowl over on purpose. You ask them to put on their jacket, and they'll throw it at you. If you ask them to sit on the potty, they run away and make in their pants.

If this is the case with your child, there are a few questions to ask yourself.

1) Has your child always been like this, or is this recent? If this is a new development, it's important to ascertain what might have changed in your child's life to elicit such a response. A new baby? Starting play group? Friction or stress in the home? Something s/he saw on television? Deal with the stress and resolve the underlying personality issues before embarking on toilet training.

2) If your child has always been resistant, ask yourself how you handle her/his contrariness. Do you feel stressed? Angry? Frustrated and helpless? Children are amazingly intuitive, and quick to sense parental frustration. They usually respond by escalating their difficult behavior. (For a more complete discussion of this, see Chapter 1, "Attitude.") They also start to feel pretty lousy about themselves. "I'm unlovable and no one loves me," they feel. So they act out more, you feel more frustrated, and round and round it goes.

You *can* interrupt this cycle by feeling more loving and accepting toward your child. "Easier said than done," you exclaim. "How can I love a child who never does what I want? Whom I can't take anywhere? Who's still wetting himself at age five?"

You can begin by focusing on the positives, rather than the negatives. There's an old saying that a person can see a glass of water as half empty or half full. You can focus on what's missing or what's present. And everyone, no matter how contrary, has some qualities that can be the objects of focus.

Consider making a list for yourself of all your child's good qualities. Don't see anything as too trivial or insignificant to record. Did she get dressed yesterday morning without being asked? Did he eat his cereal without spilling? Did she pet the cat gently? Did he kiss you good night? Then focus on these things, and praise them. Make sure your voice and facial expressions are animated and warm and truly convey your appreciation of your child's cooperation. Those areas of cooperation will be your way to restore your child's self-esteem and interrupt the cycle of blame, frustration, misbehavior, and more blame.

As your child feels you concentrating more on her/his behavior than on her/his misbehavior, s/he will begin to find that good behavior pays off. More importantly, *you'll* start to feel better, both about your child and about yourself.

3) You can use rewards and consequences more effectively now. When your child cooperates, s/he gets a round of applause, lots of hugs and kisses, and a small prize. Or perhaps a star on a chart. When s/he doesn't, there's an immediate consequence. By this I don't mean spanking or yelling, but rather the withdrawal of a privilege. If your child wets or soils him/herself, it's entirely appropriate to ask her/him to clean it up.

Inform your child that a further privilege has just been lost (perhaps the use of his model airplane for the rest of the afternoon, or perhaps the cookies you promised him as snack), and that more will be forthcoming if he doesn't clean up right away. Stand your ground firmly but calmly, realizing that your child will try the same behaviors several times until he's convinced that they no longer serve him.

And if he listens—then praise him to the hilt! If your child doesn't respond, then perhaps it's time to get some help—from a friend, clergyperson, or professional counselor.

4) Consider letting someone else toilet train your child. Some children respond rapidly and well to outsiders when their own parents have been unable to train them. An uncle, a friendly neighbor, the teenager down the block whom your child *adores,* a best friend's parent—these are all people who might be enlisted to take over the training process. Because they're outsiders, and less emotionally invested than you are, and because your child has no past history of power struggles with them, they might have quick and stress-free success.

5) If your child knows what to do in the potty but claims s/he doesn't really have to go, then set up routine bathroom times that are nonnegotiable. Your child can help you to choose those times, if s/he's willing to do so. (In fact, the more you can involve her/him, the better.) Let's say you agree that each day s/he must sit on the potty until a timer rings immediately after waking up, after breakfast, before and after lunch, before dinner, and before bed. These become part of the daily routine, regardless of your child's need to go, and are as integral as toothbrushing, eating, or changing into pajamas. Again, if your child refuses, make some other privilege contingent upon the use of the potty.

A CHILD WHO'S BEEN TRAINED TOO HARSHLY

Some children who are still in diapers when they're four or five years old are rebelling against toilet training methods tried upon them when they were younger, which were too harsh or rigid. They've learned to associate the potty with stern and unwavering rules, parental demands that seemed impossible to follow, punishments, and criticism.

It's important to realize, however, that children are quite resilient. It is unlikely that your child is permanently scarred, either in her/his relationship with you or in her/his ability to use the potty appropriately. With some warmth, love, understanding, and clear goal-setting on your part, you can renew your relationship with your child and teach her/him to use the potty.

1) Learn to forgive yourself. You acted out of the best of intentions, even if your methods were misguided. What's important is your relationship with your child *now*.

2) Talk frankly with your child, explaining how you've changed in your approaches. Indicate that you realize that her/his bodily functions are her/his domain not yours, but that sooner or later s/he will need to learn how to use the toilet or potty for these. Give her/him time, but keep your goal in mind, and set a date together with your child.

3) Follow the steps outlined in Chapter 7, "The One-Day Intensive Approach," the section on other one-day approaches.

4) If your child continues to associate you with harsh, punitive toilet training, then consider asking someone else to train her/him. (See above, "The Resistant Child.")

5) Make sure to give your child lots of praise and positive support in all areas of her/his life.

Most of all, keep loving and hoping! Don't fall into the trap of seeing your child as a hateful villain, nor as a helpless victim. S/he is neither. Don't see the situation as hopeless and grimly envision your child 10 years from now as an adolescent in diapers. Don't get caught up in blaming yourself for the past or worrying about the future. Focus on the present moment, with all its wonder and potential, and remain confident that this problem can be resolved.

9

General Tips

By now, your child is successfully and happily toilet trained—or is s/he? It's not uncommon for glitches and snags to arise somewhere along the way. This is because children are people, with minds and ideas of their own. They're not machines that will function predictably at the push of a button. (Even some machines don't always do that, as we all know!) This chapter will address some of the common problems that crop up in the toilet training process.

THE TWOS—TERRIBLE OR TERRIFIC?

The two-year-old is legend in American parenting lore for negativity. Ask a hungry two-year-old if s/he wants lunch, and you'll probably be met with a resounding "NO!" Some child-care experts call that two-year-old phase "first adolescence" because children are discovering that they are independent entities, not merely extensions of Mom and Dad. They are testing the limits of that independence.

Some parents consider the experience of dealing with a two-year-old to be a dreadful and harrowing ordeal. Others see it as a delightful challenge, and rejoice in their child's discovery of her/his own voice and will. (As Eda LeShan reminds parents in her book *When Your Child Drives You Crazy,* you will *want* your child to know how to say "no" as s/he gets older—to say no to peers who beckon with drugs, undesirable sexual behavior, cheating, and lying. S/he's simply practicing the skill on you!) How you regard your child's "no-ing" (I'm deliberately not using the word negativity because it has too many judgmental connotations) will determine whether toilet training becomes a battle of wills or a joint enterprise with you and your child acting as allies, rather than adversaries.

It is precisely because of the tendency of a two-year-old to say no that some child care experts suggest beginning toilet training when your child is age one. (See Chapter 4, "Approaches to Toilet Training.") But if you decide to start training when your child is two, or even if you started at age one, some issues of potential conflict might arise. The rest of this chapter will outline some suggestions about dealing with them, as well as discussing other issues and solutions that may crop up in the toilet training process.

CHOICES

As much as possible, try to give your child choices, rather than laying down the law or asking "yes-no" questions. In other words, don't say, "Do you have to make?" Your child—especially at age two—will probably say no, even if her/his bladder is shouting out the opposite. Instead try to incorporate a choice in your question. "Would you like to use the upstairs bathroom, or the downstairs?" Or, "Shall I help you pull down your pants, or can you do it yourself?" These questions assume that your child *will* be using the facilities, but honors her/his desire to exercise independent judgment by giving some choice.

INCORPORATE SUGGESTION TO POTTY INTO A MORE INTERESTING SUGGESTION

Again, you want to inform your child that it's time to use the bathroom without ordering her/him about and encountering a possible "no." You might include the bathroom suggestion as part of a broader plan that will capture her/his interest. "After going to the potty, we'll go to the park." "Let's put the bunny rabbit towel in the bathroom, so you can use it to dry your hands when you've made." Here, too, you're assuming that your child will use the potty, but your wording makes the towel or the park the focus, rather than the potty.

BE ALERT TO NONVERBAL SIGNALS

Observe your child carefully. Whatever the age, most children give the game away when they're trying to "hold it in." Some telltale signs are hopping back and forth from one leg to the other; covering the genital area with one or both hands; crossing the legs; and sitting down when s/he would ordinarily stand. (Some children feel that sitting down enables them to hold it in more effectively.) When you notice any of these things, then gently ask your child if s/he needs to use the bathroom. If you're dealing with a two-year-old, you might want to use some other way of suggesting the use of the bathroom, rather than a direct yes-or-no question, as discussed above.

"I *KNOW* S/HE HAS TO GO, BUT S/HE SAYS S/HE DOESN'T HAVE TO!"

You *know* Freddy's holding it in. He's dancing around, with one hand between his legs. He hasn't gone since breakfast. But when you ask him to go, he refuses.

Some children respond well to the idea of an experiment. "You don't have to make anything. Just sit and let's see if something comes out." Variations on that theme are suggesting that the child sit until the count of ten, and if nothing comes out, then s/he can get off the potty. Almost invariably, if the child *really* needs to go, then it will start coming out before you reach 10. (You might increase the interest by counting in different languages, singing the alphabet or some other favorite song.) You can set an egg timer for a minute or two (no longer) and ask her/him to sit "until the bell rings." Most children are intrigued by the ticking noise and are surprised and pleased when they hear the bell. If Freddy really needs to relieve himself, then it's almost sure to happen before the bell rings. All of these are face-saving ways for the child. They get her/him onto the toilet in a way that is interesting and stress-free, without getting into the power struggle of "I know you have to go"–"No I don't"–"Yes you do"–"No I don't."

Some children like to watch their toys using the potty first ("First it's Teddy Bear's turn, then it'll be your turn)." You can then tell them that Teddy Bear needs to use the potty, and ask them to assist. If your child isn't interested in that, or you have no toys available, then be creative with other things. One mother wriggled her index fingers, and told her daughter that the fingers had to use the potty. For several weeks after that, each time her daughter needed to make, she "took her fingers to the potty" first. She laughed as the fingers "made," and then climbed onto the potty happily.

Interesting towels, toilet paper, and soap often motivate children to use the bathroom. "Let's go say hi to the doggies on the towel." "When you're done making, you can wash your hands with the Big Bird soap." These are available in most children's stores, as well as in some super-markets.

GUIDING HANDS

Sometimes a little assistance from a pair of gentle hands conveys to your child the message that it's time to use the bathroom. I don't mean pushing or shoving, of course. Just lightly and easily touching your child on the shoulders and moving in the direction of the bathroom. If your child is one of those kids who seem to crave touch, this may be an additional factor helping her/him move toward the bathroom. Some children, however, shrink from being touched too much. In that case, you probably will want to find other alternatives.

FUNNY POSITIONS

At the beginning, your child might experiment with odd postures while using the potty or toilet. It's not uncommon for little girls to try to urinate in a standing position, for example. You don't need to rush and consult your handy Freudian textbook, trying to unearth hidden penis envy if this happens. Your daughter is simply trying out an inter-esting way of urinating. Perhaps she's trying to imitate a boy she's seen somewhere. She'll soon learn that she lacks the proper equipment to successfully urinate standing up, and will sit down. (If she insists upon standing up, and ends up splashing the seat or floor, then it's entirely appropriate to ask her to clean up after herself. No matter how young she is, you can give her a rag and she can go through the clean-up motions, even if you help by guiding her hands.)

Some children straddle the seat backward, horseback style. Others experiment with sitting on the sides. These are all perfectly normal variations on the basic theme of going in the potty or toilet and will probably be phased out rather quickly.

WASTE MATTER IS INTERESTING!

Don't be surprised if your child becomes fascinated with bathrooms and waste. It's normal for kids to inspect their productions carefully, and request to see other people's as well. This is just part of the novelty of using the potty. Once the novelty wears off, your child will probably turn her/his attention to other things, and the fascination with excreta will fade.

BATHROOM JOKES

Because of their new preoccupation with the toilet, some verbal children become fascinated by "bathroom jokes." You can sit in a car pool of preschoolers—some of whom have been trained fairly recently—and listen to them joking about their "doodies" and "pee-pees." Often, they'll pull out their entire arsenal of bathroom vocabulary—excreta and genitalia—and shout them out, amid giggles, to their friends.

The best way to handle this is by not getting shocked. The more upset or shocked you are, the more fun it'll be for your child. It would be better to ignore the words completely. Or indicate to your child, mildly and matter-of-factly, that these are bathroom words, not living room words. Some gentle distraction might help. After all, it's more interesting to draw a picture than to say "doody" one hundred times—especially if your parents don't seem to care.

FECES SMEARING

Some children take their fascination with their excreta to a rather unfortunate extreme. Unfortunate, that is, for their parents, who treasure cleanliness and hygiene. Not unfortunate for the children, who see their bowel movements as interesting playthings, and start to smear them around. In fact, Sigmund Freud, the father of modern psychology, theorized that the love that children have for playing with mud and clay is really a sublimated love for playing with their own movements. Lest you think that Freud was somewhat deranged in his bizarre notions, let me assure you that I heard this spontaneously from the lips of a four-year-old. (And take my word for it: She never opened a page of Freud in her life!)

"Do you know why I love playing with Play-Doh so much?" she asked me.

"No," I answered. "Tell me why."

"Because," she said, "I would really like to play with my BMs. But since I can't do that, I play with Play-Doh instead!"

If you come upon your child playing with feces, don't panic. Remember that your child has no judgments about waste. It's an interesting object—that's all. S/he has no understanding of hygiene and sanitation. So simply explain calmly that bowel movements are not toys. You might want to go into a little more detail with a verbal child, and discuss the concept of germs in a simple way. Explain that bowel movements belong in the toilet or potty, not on the hands, floor, or walls. Ask your child to help you clean up the mess, and be sure to provide plenty of clay or Play-Doh in the weeks ahead.

When you are discussing the matter with your child, don't use words like "yucky" or "gross" when talking about bowel movements. You don't want her/him to feel bad about what s/he did—just to understand that you don't want it done again.

REMINDERS

When your child is newly trained—and even after your child is a veteran potty user—s/he might need reminders to use the bathroom. Children become absorbed in play easily and may be reluctant to take the time to use the bathroom. They may be so engrossed in what they're doing that they are scarcely aware of their own bodily signals. A gentle reminder on your part might go a long way.

Of course, you don't want to become a nag. No one— whether age one, two, three, or adult—wants to be asked constantly, "Do you need to go to the bathroom?" Aside from the fact that your child might come to regard you as a nuisance and a nag, you communicate a sense of distrust. "You probably won't remember to go, so I have to keep reminding you." You also don't want your child to become dependent upon parental reminders to use the bathroom. Ultimately, s/he must become self-motivated. So keep your reminders to a minimum, and trust your child. As s/he gets older, and more proficient in toileting, you can phase the reminders out.

An alternative to reminders are routine trips to the bathroom. Each day at approximately the same time, you suggest a trip to the bathroom (unless your child has just recently gone). Your child comes to expect that at certain times s/he'll be going to the bathroom, and this becomes incorporated in the day. (Many nursery schools schedule "class trips" to the bathroom in this way.)

TRANSITION TO THE TOILET

Sooner or later, your child will stop using the potty and start using the toilet. For some children this happens rather early—several weeks after they've learned to use the potty, they're already clamoring to use the "real" toilet. Other children are quite content with the potty, even well into nursery school. For them, the toilet might look a little too formidable, since it's high off the ground, filled with water, and makes a loud noise.

Don't push. As Doug grows taller, the toilet will become more proportionate to his size. As he gets more used to the bathroom, you can flush more often until he's accustomed to the noise. You can also get toilet seat adaptors. (See Chapter 3, "Choosing a Potty.") with steps, which will make the "hole" smaller and less scary-looking. Allow your child to climb up and down the steps and get used to that, with the lid closed, before doing so with an open lid. You can teach her/him to balance and hold on to the toilet seat, too.

When your child finally *does* use the toilet, be lavish in your praise. S/he's just reached another milestone! The potty can be retired until the next child comes along.

You might want to keep your potty around a little longer, however. If you have a house full of guests, and the bathrooms are constantly in use, your child might use a potty in another room, if there's an urgent need to go. The potty is also handy for travel. (See below.) But if these situations don't arise, the potty can be consigned to the attic. Congratulations!

TRAVEL

Travel presents its own set of challenges and issues. There may be no bathroom for many miles of highway; the bathrooms in trains, buses, or airplanes may have long lines waiting to get in and may be dirty once you get there. You may have other children with you, and finding a bathroom in a crowded department store or amusement park may be complicated and inconvenient.

Try as much as possible to have your child use the bathroom *immediately* before leaving the house. If s/he used it an hour ago, suggest another try. Even if you hear the inevitable "But I don't have to go!" be firm in insisting that it's household policy for everyone to use the bathroom before going out on the road.

While part of the training process involves encouraging your child to feel comfortable using the outdoors when necessary, rather than holding it in if no bathroom is available, some children may feel reluctant to do so. They're not used to squatting on the ground, with the grass tickling their behinds, and as much as they have to make, the urine simply won't come out. They're too tense. You also don't want to encourage them to make bowel movements outdoors on the ground. So it helps to carry a lidded potty with you in the car. If your child needs to make, you can pull over to the side of the road, and your child can use the potty there. The lid prevents spills and keeps odors confined as much as possible.

Don't have your child use the potty while the car is in motion. It's unsafe for a young child to be unstrapped and outside the car seat while the car is moving. It's also more conducive to spills and mess.

If you've followed some of the suggestions in Chapter 5, then your child is familiar with and comfortable using many bathrooms. Yet, many public rest rooms are quite dirty and unsanitary. Disinfectant sprays, available in pharmacies and some supermarkets, will sanitize the toilet seats. It's always a good idea to teach your child to cover the toilet seat if s/he's sitting down. You can buy toilet seat covers for the purpose, or use toilet paper.

Discuss with your child ahead of time if the bathroom is going to be dramatically different from what s/he's used to. If you're going on an airplane, for example, or to a camping site, prepare your child for what the bathrooms will look and feel like. (Picture books might be available from the library for the purpose.) And while using a potty in an airplane aisle might be difficult and inconsiderate to other passengers, you can certainly bring it almost everywhere else and use it if your child seems reluctant to use the public bathroom.

If your child asks to use the bathroom, try to be as accommodating as possible, even if it's inconvenient. Children's urinary systems are less mature than those of adults, and they're more likely to react to excitement by needing to go to the bathroom. Remember, travel is exciting for children. Their excitement may take the form of extra urination.

If your child refused to use the bathroom before leaving the house, or sat without producing anything, try to restrain yourself from the accusatory "I *told* you to go before we left home!" If you feel irritated, wait until that feeling has subsided, then explain to your child that this was the very situation you wanted to avoid and that next time s/he *must* use the bathroom before leaving. Next time, you can remind your child of this trip and how it was interrupted because of her/his refusal to use the bathroom before leaving. Remember, too, that you don't want to reward your child by giving her/him a lot of extra attention for refusing to go. Scolding and lecturing are forms of attention. Your child commands the floor—and you. So be as bland as you can be. But remain firm: Next time, you'll accept no "nos."

Keep baby wipes handy in the car. (Don't bury them under a pile of clothes in your suitcase or at the bottom of the trunk!) They're great for bottom-wiping, as well as for hand washing when there's no sink.

If there's a long line waiting for the bathroom, most people will understand if you request to go ahead of others. You can explain that your child has just been trained and urgently needs to use the bathroom. Most people will be quite sympathetic, smile graciously, and allow you to go ahead.

If you're in a city, you might ask to use a restaurant bathroom, even if you're not eating there. Again, most people are very sympathetic to the needs of a parent, and of a newly trained child, and the management is likely to allow you to use the bathroom with no problems.

Some stores have a policy forbidding customers from using bathrooms. If polite explanations don't help, and the salespeople remain rigid in adhering to this rule, then ask to speak to the store manager or owner. (A jovial threat might go a long way, too. "S/he's just learned to use the toilet last week. You wouldn't want it to come out onto your floor, would you?") The key is to be pleasant, but also assertive.

AVOID WORDS LIKE "STINKY" OR "DISGUSTING"

When toileting your child—and this actually begins early, when changing diapers—avoid expressions of disgust or distaste at the excreta. Holding your nose, grimacing, and saying "Pee-yoo!" convey to your child that what comes out of the body is distasteful. Some children might then feel *themselves* to be distasteful for having produced something that can elicit such a strong response. You want to build your child's self-esteem, not ruin it! If your child has produced urine or feces—whether in the potty, or in underpants—deal with it without expressions of revulsion.

DISCOVERING THE ANATOMY

Some children discover their genitals for the first time when they're being toilet trained. In our culture, children are covered by diapers and clothing almost all the time, except when they're being diapered or when they're in the bathtub. In the tub, they're usually so busy with the water and the bath toys that their own bodies are less interesting. But while they're sitting on the potty or toilet, focusing on the productions of their private parts, those parts become quite interesting for them. Little boys also hold their penises while urinating so as to aim properly. It's not uncommon to find them playing with their genitals while they're pottying. And even when they're not, they've become aware of a new and interesting part of their body, and they'll use other opportunities to explore it.

Children cannot see why these parts of the body should be kept hidden. To a child, a penis or a vagina is no more private than a toe or an ear. Children don't have the same beliefs and judgments about privacy as adults do. And believe me, if your child's toes had always been covered and were suddenly made available, s/he would spend hours playing with toes!

As with bathroom jokes, the novelty of the genitals will wear off, and your child will focus on other things—unless you make it an issue. If you believe that touching yourself is a sin, or will lead to blindness or insanity (as was believed generations ago), and if you react with threats, anger, or punishment, you might have a deleterious effect on your child's self-image, as well as her/his sexuality. You'll also be "juicing" the child's behavior by responding in an interesting, albeit angry way. Your best bet is to react blandly and calmly. Either ignore the whole thing or tell your child that genitals are private and to be touched only in the privacy of her/his room or the bathroom. Some gentle distraction might help. You might give your child an interesting toy to hold while using the potty, for example. Use a gentle reminder, offer distractions, and keep in mind that this preoccupation with genitals will fade.

If genital playing has become persistent, and your child

is unable to be distracted and has become excessively focused upon her/his genitals, then it needs to be investigated a little further. The old dictum "Forbidden fruit is sweetest" might apply here. Have you created a prohibitive atmosphere around these things, thus making the genitals more interesting than they need to be?

If this isn't the case, ask yourself whether your child might just be bored. Perhaps this is the time to consider nursery school or play group, or to buy a couple of new toys, or to spend some extra time bringing her/him to the park or playing in the backyard.

If your child's schedule is full and engaging, then perhaps there's some source of stress in her/his life. Beginning nursery, a new baby-sitter, a new sibling, for example, might be stressful. Some children respond to stress by reaching for their private parts.

You might also investigate the possibility of sexual abuse. While sexual abuse is relatively rare, it *does* sometimes happen. Day care workers, baby-sitters, neighbors, friends' parents, and even family members sometimes use their close contact with children for exploitative purposes. One telltale symptom is a child's inordinate desire to play with her/his genitals. If you do suspect that your child has been abused, try in a calm and nonjudgmental manner to invite your child to tell you about it. Without alarming your child, tell her or him that you will take steps to prevent further abuse. Consult the Child Protection Agency, a school counselor, or a state or local abuse prevention office for full information on how to handle child abuse.

Lastly, it's worth checking out whether your child has some fear connected with the genitals. For example, it occasionally happens that when a little boy is surrounded by numerous sisters and no brothers he becomes afraid of losing his penis and becoming like "one of the girls." The reverse also happens. One little girl I know was afraid of toilet monsters and refused to go unaccompanied to the bathroom until she was six years old. It turned out that she thought she'd been born with a penis and someone had cut it off and given it to her next-door-neighbor's boy, who was about her age. Apparently she was afraid that a monster would rise from the toilet and cut off some more. In both of these cases, the children saw their genitals as objects needing protection—especially in the bathroom.

THE SKELETON IN THE CLOSET

Some children are aware that excretion is a private thing to do—but they choose rather innovative places to carry out this activity. They'll squat in closets, garages, and corners to produce their bowel movements and utterly refuse to put them in the potty or toilet. One of my daughters had a favorite place, a little nook behind the television set at my mother's house.

This may be bewildering to you. After all, if your child already understands that elimination is a private act, why won't s/he use the bathroom, for heaven's sake?

One reason might be fear of the bathroom. The subject of bathroom fear is dealt with extensively below ("Bathroom Fears"), so we won't go into it here.

Some children are simply noncomformists and can be expected to find an original way to carry out many of their activities. Others are creatures of habit. Perhaps they were once playing behind the couch in the den when the need to move their bowels overtook them. It didn't seem like such a bad place to go at all! So next time, they tried it again. Soon just being there stimulated their colon, through a conditioned response, and voilà! A new toilet has been created.

Whatever the reason, you certainly don't want feces deposited anywhere except the potty or toilet. So explain this to your child. Again, make sure your attitude is loving and accepting, rather than angry or judgmental. Tell your child that the only place for excretion is the bathroom. If you encounter reluctance or fear, allow your child to wear a diaper at first—just so long as the site of excretion is moved to the bathroom. Then be vigilant. If your child approaches that favorite "making spot," whisk her/him away to the bathroom.

Once your child is accustomed to using the bathroom, then tell her/him that it's time to sit on the potty, keeping the lid closed. Again, a diaper can be used—but excretion must take place on the potty. Once this is routine, ask your child to remove the diaper or pants. By this time, s/he should be comfortable enough in the bathroom to do so without difficulty.

Some children don't need all these intermediate steps. They're comfortable immediately with using the potty or toilet instead of the corner or closet. Just remember to be aware of when your child approaches the former "making spot." Remind her/him that this isn't the place to make, and take her/him to the bathroom.

Some children respond well to being allowed to make on a newspaper on the bathroom floor. This seems to meet the same need as their private "making spot" did. It is usually a transition of a couple of weeks before they outgrow this stage and are willing to use the potty.

Some children choose unusual excretory locations as a response to pressure. They feel that this gives them control and provides a private, pressure-free situation in which they're not "on display" or required to perform for someone else. Ask yourself whether this might apply to your child. Has toilet training become a pressured experience for your child rather than a smooth, easy, stress-free process? Are you, your spouse, or perhaps someone else in your child's life, demanding too much? Is there some other area in your life in which your child feels pressured?

If too much pressure seems to be the problem, then try to ease up as much as possible. This might not be the time to teach how to use cutlery, for example, or insist on a clean room. Assure your child of your ongoing love and of your respect for *her/his* choices. Make a point of trying to give her/him as much autonomy as possible. Some extra time and attention will go a long way, too.

BATHROOM FEARS

Sometimes even the most intelligent, well-adjusted child becomes frightened of the bathroom. This can lead to reactions ranging from mild reluctance to downright refusal to enter the door under any circumstances. Some children insist upon having a parent in the room, way past the age when parental assistance is really necessary. Others become "closet excretors" (see above, "The Skeleton in the Closet"). Still others hold back their bowel movements until their rectum becomes impacted with unexcreted feces (see below, "Constipation" and also Chapter 11, "Encopresis").

Children may have a variety of fears associated with the bathroom. Perhaps they're afraid of the flushing noise. Perhaps they saw their movements whisked away and they're afraid that this will happen to *them* as well. Young children do not yet have a concept of relative size. They don't understand that they're too big to go down the drain.

If your child has ever had a scary experience in the bathroom, the room may continue to hold frightening associations. I'm not talking here about a major trauma, necessarily, but even something relatively "minor" from an adult point of view. For example, if your child ever fell in the bathroom, if the potty ever toppled over, if s/he scraped her/himself on the urine deflector, passed a hard, painful movement, or experienced burning during urination as a result of, say, a urinary tract infection; if a sibling jumped out from behind the shower curtain and yelled "Boo!"—all these might leave vestiges of fear, long after the actual experience has been forgotten.

Don't dismiss your child's fears as silly or nonsense. From your adult perspective, you realize that the fears are groundless. But they feel very real to your child. Accord her/him the respect you yourself would like if you shared a concern with a dear friend. Listen openly, and acknowledge that you understand. Then try to deal with the fear itself.

If your child is afraid of falling, let her/him practice using the potty or toilet, even when it's not time to excrete. Hold her/his hand if necessary. And compliment her/him on her/his physical coordination and sense of balance in other areas as well ("Wow, look at you climb up those monkey bars! All those steps, and you didn't fall once! I bet you could do that in the bathroom as well.") The more self-confident your child feels, the less fear of falling there'll be.

If your child is afraid of the noise of the toilet flushing, then drop the subject of toilet training for a few weeks and spend some time playing with different noises. Use your voices and experiment with shouts, grunts, screams, and other noises. Try to get hold of musical instruments—some loud and some soft—and let your child experience different noises. Use the vacuum cleaner, blender, radio, cuckoo clock, or any other interesting source of noise on hand. The flushing of the toilet is just one noise in a whole array you'll be exploring together. By the time a few weeks have passed, your child should be well over the fear of noise, and you can reintroduce the potty and the bathroom.

If your child is afraid of going down the drain, you may want to spend some weeks exploring together the concept of relative size. The bath is a wonderful place to begin. Place several large toys there, and show how they don't go down the drain when the water is let out. One mother even tried to flush a doll down the toilet. Her daughter saw that the doll was too large to go down the little hole, and she stopped being afraid. You can use toys as well, showing how large ones fit into small ones, but small ones can't fit into large ones. In a couple of weeks, try pottying again.

Some children become afraid of the potty when they've experienced pain using it. If, for example, they've passed a particularly hard, painful movement, or if their urine burned when voiding, they may blame the bathroom. If they're verbal, you can explain in simple terms that they had a little sickness in the part of their body that produces BMs or pee-pees. Remind them of other illnesses they might have had—colds, ear infections, and so on. You might even point to their knees and remind them of that time when they fell and had a boo-boo and how it healed up. Explain that their bodies have healed in this area as well and that defecation and urination probably won't hurt any more. Be patient! Sometimes it takes a little while to overcome a fear.

Meanwhile, use every opportunity to bring home this point to your child. When you change a diaper, or a wet pair of training pants, draw her/his attention to the fact that producing the wetness or the BM didn't hurt. Suggest an experiment next time. "Let's see how it goes when you try to make in the potty." A reward often helps. "I know you're going to be very brave to try the potty again. I'm so proud of you! Would you like a piggyback ride when you've made?"

It might also help to rub a tiny bit of Vaseline or Desitin ointment over the appropriate area. Even if there's no actual physical damage there, your child's awareness of protective medicine will give her/him courage to try to void or evacuate again. This can be called the Band-Aid effect—children seem to feel remarkably better when a Band-Aid is put over their scrapes, even though it has no actual healing properties. Once s/he has successfully urinated or eliminated without pain or discomfort, s/he'll be able to do so again and again, and the fear will disappear.

If some other scary experience has befallen your child when in the bathroom—let's say an older sibling jumped out from the shower stall and startled her/him—then try to get your child to talk about it. If s/he's not yet sufficiently verbal, then try what psychologists call the desensitization approach. First encourage your child to think about the bathroom and visualize it in her/his mind's eye. You can do so with photographs, books, or drawing pictures together. If s/he seems able to do so without becoming frightened, then ask her/him to come into the bathroom with clothes on, and just stay there for a while. If s/he refuses, then ask her/him to sit outside the bathroom and peer inside. Again, a small reward might serve as an incentive to try something that is being seen as frightening. Once this has been accomplished, then try bringing her/him into the bathroom. Show her/him around the room. Step in and out of the tub, shower, or whatever other equipment you have in there. Open and close the medicine chest, vanity cabinets, hamper, or other items to demonstrate that there is nothing scary lurking within.

Don't push your child to use the potty right away. Allow her/him first to spend a few days becoming accustomed to the bathroom. Eventually, you can suggest trying out the potty again.

Another alternative if your child is scared of the bathroom as a result of some frightening experience that happened in there is to move the potty elsewhere for a little while. Your child will continue using the potty for urine or bowel movements, while you work on the bathroom fears.

Keep moving the potty closer and closer to the bathroom as your child becomes more comfortable, and eventually move it back in.

If your child is experiencing some prolonged fear and doesn't seem to be responding to your efforts, then consider professional counseling. Begin by discussing the situation with a pediatrician, a school counselor, or a social worker who will help you assess the degree of the problem and advise you on how to proceed.

CONSTIPATION

We often think of constipation as something that affects primarily senior citizens. But the fact is that many children suffer from constipation as well. Before we examine the various reasons for this, let's first define what constipation is—and what it isn't.

Some people believe that children should have at least one bowel movement every day, and that if they don't, this means that they are constipated. Today's doctors say that this is a myth. Bowel patterns vary from child to child. Some children move their bowels a few times a day. Others move their bowels once every few days. Both are normal.

Constipation occurs when the movements are hard and difficult to pass. The child knows they're there and feels the need to eliminate them but is unable to do so. S/he may sit for a long time and squeeze, with varying degrees of success. Or s/he may give up, go back to playing, and hope that "next time I try it'll really come out."

Prolonged sitting and excessive squeezing may lead to hemorrhoids. (Yes, they occasionally happen even to children.) When the stool eventually *does* come out, it's so hard that it scrapes the wall of the anus, which can cause anal fissures (see below, "Anal Fissures"). If the child decides to defer the whole process until later, the bowel can become impacted, causing discomfort, and loss of muscle tone in the colon and rectum. (see Chapter 11, "Encopresis").

Your first port of call in case of frequent constipation should be your doctor. There are a number of physical reasons for constipation that should be ruled out before you proceed further on your own. Other than gastrointenstinal diseases, which are pretty rare, a common cause of constipation is allergy. Undetected food allergies (especially dairy, but others as well) can often lead to constipation. Your pediatrician can refer you to an allergist for testing. Or you can try your own informal testing program by putting your child on an elimination diet for a few weeks. An excellent book outlining a program that will ascertain whether your child has allergies is *Food Allergies* by Sarah Bingham and Neil Orenstein.

If you do find your child to be allergic to a food—especially something that is central to her/his diet, such as milk—don't just cut the food out "cold turkey." Talk to your doctor or to a nutritionist about how to ensure that your child will receive the proper amount of protein, calcium, vitamins, and minerals from other foods that s/he *does* tolerate.

An even more common cause for constipation is poor diet. The typical American diet is not conducive to maximum intestinal health. Refined sugars, peanut butter, white flour, refined cereals, chocolate, sweets, and diary products are some of the staples of the American child's diet. All these are very binding foods. If your child suffers from constipation, then cut back or even eliminate some of these foods. Increase foods that are high in fiber. Whole grain products—cereal with bran for breakfast, a whole wheat sandwich for lunch, and brown rice, or some other whole grain side dish for dinner—for starters. Fresh fruits and vegetables are excellent as well. All vegetables will help, but especially broccoli, cauliflower, lettuce, peas, and beans. When serving fruit, stone fruits (cherries, peaches, plums, and so on.) seem to loosen stool more than other fruits. Dried prunes and raisins are known for their laxative effects. Bananas, apples, and applesauce seem to have a binding effect and should be kept to a minimum or avoided, although apple juice can help produce the desired results.

"But my child won't *touch* vegetables!" This is an all-too-common complaint of parents, who find their children's fingers inching toward the potato chips, as they push away the spinach on their plates.

If Frankie refuses vegetables and fruits, then begin by talking to him. Help him to understand *why* you want him to eat these "yucky" foods. Chances are that he's pretty uncomfortable with his stuffed up bowel and would be delighted to try something that will help. Explain that these foods will help the BMs to become softer and to come out more smoothly.

You can also refuse to serve his favorite foods until he's had a substantial serving of whole grains, vegetables, and fruits with every meal. If he announces dramatically, "I'd rather starve!" then stick to your guns! The old saying "hunger is the best source" is applicable here. There's nothing like hunger pangs to draw a child to the table and motivate her/him to sample even the most unappealing looking food. And most children really *enjoy* these foods once they get used to them.

Prepare a snack plate of whole grain crackers, sliced fruits, and vegetables for after school, or while your child is watching TV (a notorious snack time). Leave the cut up carrot sticks, broccoli florets, celery, cucumber, and pepper on the kitchen table for the kids to grab as they run in and out of the house to play. Grapes are easy to carry around, and make a delicious (and highly laxative) snack food.

Make sure your child is drinking enough, even when s/he doesn't seem to be thirsty. Lack of sufficient body fluid contributes to hard stool. Water is fine, of course, but in this situation fruit juices are better. (Fig and prune juice are renowned for their laxative qualities.) If Barbara doesn't like to gulp down a large glass of juice, then supply her with a canteen, Thermos, or box drink, which can be sipped as she goes about her playing.

Exercise is very important for the healthy maintenance of the bowel. So try to limit the amount of time your child spends sitting in front of the television or VCR, and encourage lots of outdoor play—basketball, bike riding, playing tag with the neighbors, and so on. If your child's school is deficient in the number of hours devoted to gym and recess, and your child is sitting for long periods of time, then speak to the school administration and other parents. Perhaps some additional opportunities for exercise can be introduced. Teachers can be asked to provide short breaks even during class time, in which children can walk around and do some stretch exercises before returning to their studies. If the school isn't open to these ideas, then try to initiate an after-school exercise program—ball, swimming, or some other interesting activity for your child and her/his friends. This will yield wonderful health benefits for all children, even those who don't suffer from constipation.

If none of these ideas are effective, your doctor may suggest a mild stool softener or laxative. It's not a good idea to administer laxatives on your own, because your child might become dependent on them. Speak to your doctor and see if a laxative can be included in a broader plan to help remedy your child's bowel habits.

For a further discussion of constipation, see Chapter 11, "Encopresis."

ANAL FISSURES

An anal fissure is a tiny tear in the anus wall. It usually occurs as a result of being scraped or torn by an excessively hard bowel movement and sometimes causes blood in the stool.

If your child is having hard stool, then follow some of the suggestions for constipation. Meanwhile, put a little Vaseline or Desitin on the fissure after each movement and at bedtime until it heals up. If your child gives you enough advance notice, then put some on right before the movement. That way the movement won't irritate an already irritated area as it passes through.

DIARRHEA

As with constipation, many myths about diarrhea abound. Some people feel that if a child has more than one bowel movement a day, s/he is suffering from diarrhea. This isn't the case at all. Diarrhea is characterized by loose, watery stool, even if there's no frequency.

Diarrhea is often caused by a stomach virus. When that happens, it's usually, though not necessarily, accompanied by vomiting, abdominal pain, and fever. Consult your doctor as to how to treat this condition. Medical advice may include taking your child off all solid foods and keeping her/him on a liquid diet only until it clears up. Your doctor may recommend something called Pedialyte, a fluid that maintains the balance of electrolytes in the body, which can be upset by bouts of diarrhea. Your doctor may suggest a diet high in binding foods, such as white bread, bananas, grated apple, and oatmeal. If necessary, medication might be necessary to slow up the diarrhea. Remember, even though you might dismiss the symptoms as just a stomach virus, in a young child these symptoms *can* be quite dangerous and should definitely be brought to the attention of a doctor!

If your child has had a virus, or has suffered from diarrhea for some other reason, s/he may have had difficulty holding in bowel movements. Accidents are very common under these circumstances, especially in a newly trained child. Be reassuring and comforting. Explain to the child that it's very hard for people to hold in their BMs when they're sick, and that as soon as s/he gets better, s/he'll be able to do so again without any problem. You might consider putting your child back in a diaper or in disposable training pants for this time. Again, explain that the illness has created a special circumstance, which will be accommodated by diapers until s/he is feeling better. Encourage your child, however, to use the potty as much as possible, and not to rely upon the diaper.

If your child is taking antibiotics, be aware that diarrhea is often a common side effect.

As with constipation, chronic or persistent diarrhea should be checked out first with a pediatrician. There are a number of illnesses that might give rise to it. As with constipation, allergies are often a prime offender. Follow the steps recommended above (see ''Constipation'') to ascertain whether your child has allergies and to deal with the situation if s/he does.

Some children simply have what's called ''toddler diarrhea.'' For no clear reason, their movements are frequent and loose and often arrive without much warning. So work with your child, sensitizing her/him to even subtle signals that a movement is about to take place. This may be difficult with a preverbal child and may have to wait until you and your child can sit down and discuss what it feels like inside her/his body right before a movement. Encourage routine trips to the bathroom, even when s/he doesn't feel the need—especially before going someplace where there isn't a toilet immediately accessible. Even a short trip in the car, a visit to a large department store, or a walk around the block is potentially problematic because the toilet isn't right where the child is. While your child is still in the early training stages, consider having her/him wear a plastic shell over the training pants or wear disposable training pants when you go out. And don't worry. Toddler diarrhea usually eases up by itself as the child's digestive system matures.

INFECTIONS

Urinary tract infections are pretty common in children. Some symptoms to be alert for are: pain; burning, or stinging upon voiding; unusual frequency; itching; cloudy urine; blood in the urine; an unusually strong or foul odor from the urine; urine leakage into the underwear; sudden, urgent needs to urinate; unexplained fever; urinary incontinence in a child who's already been trained; bed-wetting; inability to learn to urinate in the potty. Your doctor will take a urine culture to determine whether your child has an infection.

Urinary tract infections are much more common in girls than in boys. The most common reason is failure to wipe correctly (see Chapter 5, "First Steps)". The urethra is much shorter in girls than in boys, so a girl who wipes incorrectly introduces fecal material to her urinary tract, and the fecal bacteria lead to infection. Occasionally, it's caused by touching the vaginal area with dirty hands. So continue to educate your daughter in hygienic wiping practices, and make sure she washes her hands well after play, if she's going to touch her genitals.

The most common treatment for urinary tract infection is antibiotics. Your doctor may also suggest drinking cranberry juice or some other juice high in vitamin C.

Because urinary tract infections are pretty rare in boys, your pediatrician may suggest a urological workup to see if your son has any structural abnormalities. Doctors usually hold off recommending such a workup for girls, unless they have recurrent infections.

Some girls contract vaginal yeast infections as a result of being on antibiotics. These are treated with special creams or suppositories.

Girls don't have a monopoly on infections. There is an infection called balinitis, which uncircumcised boys sometimes develop under their foreskin. Keep your eyes open for signs of redness and pain in urination. Sometimes this infection is treated with antibiotics. But the most important treatment involves greater attentiveness to hygiene. Teach your son to gently pull back his foreskin as far as it will go, so as to clean underneath. Make sure to dry it afterward.

DELIBERATE WETTING OR SOILING

Every so often, children experiment with deliberate wetting or soiling. For some kids, it's an interesting experiment. Children are little scientists. They are constantly finding out about their world by trying to understand what will move the people around them. To this end, they try out all sorts of different actions.

For other children, deliberate wetting or soiling is an expression of anger. They know that Mom and Dad don't want their urine or bowel movements on the living room floor, but they're mad! "Let Mom and Dad deal with this! They sure deserve it!"

For yet other children, this is a ploy to gain their parents' attention. Mom is busy on the telephone and has been ignoring Tommy for half an hour. That little brown pile on the kitchen floor will get her off the phone pretty fast! Or perhaps Dad is busy giving the new baby a bottle. This should get his attention in a hurry!

If you suspect that your child is deliberately wetting or soiling, then there are a few steps you can take.

1) Make sure that it is, indeed, deliberate. Perhaps your child has an infection or virus and couldn't reach the bathroom on time. Perhaps s/he needs a few extra reminders, and simply forgot to go until it was too late. Perhaps s/he drank an unusually large amount or ate too many raisins. If it was really an accident, you don't want to treat it as if it were done on purpose.

2) If you are convinced that your child did this on purpose, then don't let it push your buttons. Your child *wants* you to react (see Chapter 1, "Attitude"). Your anger is, paradoxically, a reward and is exactly what your child is looking for. If you *are* angry, don't show it. Try as best as possible to respond blandly and calmly.

3) Don't rush right away to clean it up. That, too, is a reward. Mom and Dad are hopping to my command! Insist that your child clean it up. This is not a punishment but rather a natural consequence of her/his actions. If your child is too young to do an effective job, then guide her/his hands through the motions. Make the experience as reward-free as possible. While you want to encourage your child to assist in household cleanup by making it interesting, this isn't the time for that. Singing cleanup songs, putting on music, or telling stories is fine when you're cleaning up the kitchen or putting away toys. Cleaning up a deliberate accident, on the other hand, should be as boring as you can make it. If possible, don't even reward the child with your undivided attention. Continue that phone conversation, or manufacture something to talk to your spouse about while you supervise your child's cleanup.

If Alex deliberately wets or soils more than once, then examine your relationship with him. Is he angry? What could he be angry about? Talk to him about it. Try to teach him different means to express his feelings—through talking, drawing, punching a pillow, and so on. Teach him as well that anger is a choice, and help him to find alternatives.

If Flossie is wetting on purpose, ask yourself: Is she getting enough attention and time with you and your spouse? Have you been unusually preoccupied with work, social involvement, or a new baby? Try to set aside extra time for her. It would help if this could be private time—just you and her. Private times needn't be expensive trips to zoos or amusement parks, although these are wonderful and fun. They needn't be out-of-the-house trips to parks, libraries or ball games, although these are terrific ways to share and spend time as well. You can set aside some time—say, 15 to 30 minutes—each night that Flossie knows will be *her* time. She can choose what she wants to do with the time: play, color, talk, listen to music, watch TV together. This should go a long way in alleviating her sense of not getting enough of your attention. As busy as you might be, and as hectic as some households can become, try to focus your entire attention on your child when you talk to her/him.

"I'VE GOT TO GO TO THE BATHROOM—AGAIN!"

Urinary frequency (without medical cause) may also be an attempt to gain some extra attention. This is especially true for very young children, who still need some assistance in the bathroom. The suggestions above will help you deal with children who are seeking more attention.

There are other reasons for frequency. Rare as it may be, some children who have been sexually molested experience frequency. This is due either to local irritation or to the fact that the child's attention has been drawn excessively to the genital area. When exploring whether this might be the case, don't ask leading questions ("Did someone touch you in your private parts?"). Try to ask open-ended questions ("Why do you think you have to make so often? Does this happen at school, too? What does your teacher do?'' And so on). If you seriously suspect sexual molestation, then seek counseling at once. A competent counselor is trained to ferret out information from your child without putting ideas into her/his head and to help your child deal with the experience.

Some children develop urinary frequency as a result of lack of exercise. Their bodies are not being sufficiently challenged, and the energy that is produced by the metabolism of food is not burned off. As a result, they can become tense, and the tension might find a target organ: the bladder. Interestingly, the frequency gives their bodies the opportunity to do what they most need: get up and move around. As they urinate more frequently, the bladder wall becomes inflamed and irritated; and the more irritated the bladder wall, the more the child needs to urinate. And so a cycle is created.

You can interrupt the cycle by encouraging your child to relax at the end of urination and make sure the bladder is *completely* empty. Even more important, make sure your child gets plenty of vigorous exercise on a daily basis.

If these suggestions don't help, then consult your doctor.

Stress might also lead to excessive frequency. A new baby, the beginning of school, a family illness, or family friction, for example, might lead to a stressed child. If your child is urinating frequently, and medical causes have been ruled out, then investigate whether there is some stress in her/his life. Try to talk to her/him about it, preferably in private. If you are unable to uncover what this stress might be, or don't know how you can help, then consider involving someone else. Children often open up to others more than to their own parents. A caring family member—a much loved grandparent, aunt, or cousin—might be able to lend a compassionate ear and get to the root of what's bothering your child. A dear family friend, clergyperson, or teacher might also be able to help. An objective individual will also help you decide if professional counseling would be helpful and advise you on the steps to take.

TO DIAPER OR NOT TO DIAPER?

If your child has many accidents, should you return to diapers? Opinions abound among the child-care experts. Some say that switching to training pants is an irrevocable decision, and returning to diapers would be confusing to the child. Worse, it could communicate a sense of failure to the child who's been proud of her/his success.

Others feel differently. They feel that a child who's constantly having accidents is simply not ready for training pants yet. Pushing a child into pants before s/he is ready might create an unnecessarily pressured situation and will lead to a sense of failure, because the child will feel unable to measure up and do what's expected.

There is no single right answer. If you feel your child is really ready for training pants despite the continued accidents, then you might want to keep her/him in pants, while investigating the cause of these accidents. While you go through your detective work, ruling out medical or psychological reasons, it might help to keep a plastic shell over the underpants, to minimize leakage. Reassure your child, too, that s/he isn't a failure if there is an accident. This is all part of the learning process. As s/he grows up control will become easier and s/he will stay dry.

If you decide to revert to diapers for a while, then assure your child that this is not a failure on her/his part. Put it to her in a matter-of-fact way, free of blame, shame, or judgments. ''It seems that you're not quite ready for underpants yet. Let's go back to diapers for a little while, and then we'll try underpants again.''

Whatever you decide to do, your attitude of love, accep-

tance, and confidence that your child *will* move on to successfully dry underwear will be crucial in building your
child's self-esteem and understanding of what's going on.

REGRESSION

Sometimes a fully trained child suddenly regresses and
begins wetting or soiling again. If your child does this, then
begin by taking a trip to your pediatrician, who will rule
out medical problems. If there is no medical reason, then
investigate whether your child is under stress (see above,
"To Diaper or not to Diaper?"). Regression is very common when a new baby is born (both because some children
feel the addition of a new sibling to be a stressful experience, and because some children try to imitate the baby,
who still makes in diapers); when a child is separated from
her/his parents; during hospitalization; if parents are undergoing a divorce; or if there is an illness or death in the
family. Children may also feel scared of less obvious
things—a bully down the block, a mean teacher, a piano
recital.

If your child is going through a period of regression, then
treat her/him with kindness and understanding—but also
with firmness. Punishments, scolding, shaming, and blaming certainly won't help and will even be counterproductive. But too much "there, there, honey" when the child
has wet will give the child an undesired reward and will
reinforce the wetting.

It's best to treat these accidents calmly and matter-of-
factly. It is appropriate for your child to be responsible for
helping to clean up the mess. Again, this isn't punitive. We
are all responsible for cleaning up after ourselves, and there
is no reason why children shouldn't learn this lesson early.

Explore with your child why s/he thinks this is happening. If you can't uncover the source of stress or provide

adequate help in dealing with it, then consult a professional counselor.

REFERENCES AND SUGGESTIONS FOR FURTHER READING

Bingham, Sarah and Ornstein, Neil. *Food Allergies: How to Tell if You Have Them and What to Do About Them if You Do.* New York: Putnam, 1987.

Caplan, Frank and Caplan, Theresa. *The Second Twelve Months of Life: Your Baby's Growth Month by Month.* New York: Bantam Books, 1977.

Fraiberg, Selma. *The Magic Years.* New York: Charles Scribner's Sons, 1959.

Leach, Penelope. *Your Baby and Child From Birth to Age Five.* New York: Knopf, 1978.

LeShan, Eda. *When Your Child Drives You Crazy.* New York: St. Martin's Press, 1985.

Spock, Benjamin. *Baby and Child Care* (revised edition). New York: E. P. Dutton, 1985.

10

Defining and Preventing Bed-wetting

- James is an alert, active eleven-year-old. He likes baseball and computers. He enjoys playing with his friends. He would love to join them in an overnight hike this summer. But he doesn't dare. James has a secret. He still wets his bed at night.
- "I was never so embarrassed in all my life!" exclaims Mrs. Johnson. "I gave Sarah permission to go to a slumber party, and the next morning, her bed, her sheets, her nightclothes—everything was all wet. Her poor hostess had to deal with urine-soaked linens. It's not like she's a baby anymore. She's five years old!"
- "My son Bobby has never woken up dry in his life, and he's already four years old! We must be doing something wrong!"

Do any of these sound familiar? If you're nodding your head, then be comforted: Bed-wetting is much more common than you think. It is estimated that one-third of the three-year-olds in this country still wet their beds at night. Among four-year-olds, the number is only slightly smaller—a quarter are bed-wetters. Even among older children—six or seven years old—approximately one-seventh of them continue to have nighttime accidents.

Because bed-wetting—technically termed ''nocturnal enuresis''—is so common among young children, pediatricians today do not even begin to use the label until a child reaches six years old. Before then, occasional and even regular nocturnal urination is considered within the range of normal and not a major cause for concern.

But you as a parent might be quite concerned. You're marching to the sink or the washing machine, laden with wet linens, wondering whether this will *ever* stop. Here are some suggestions for approaching bed-wetting.

ATTITUDE

Bed-wetters have been judged, blamed, shamed, and even abused by parents and educators throughout history. Prior to the twentieth century, people added bizarre, even dangerous items to children's food in an attempt to curb nocturnal urination. They subjected children to hot or cold baths, enemas, nerve tonics, tight bandaging of the penis, and a host of other harsh and ineffective treatments. Children have been beaten and ridiculed for their lack of control. More recently, some parents have taken to hanging out the wet sheets on the porch for the neighborhood to see. And even parents who do not publicly humiliate their child often spew sharp and cutting comments in private.

As we discussed in Chapter 1, ''Attitude,'' judgmentalism is misplaced in parenting. Your child is doing the best s/he can to make sense of the world around her/him. And if s/he sometimes behaves in ways that differ from what you want for her, then this is a cry for love, not for anger. This would be true in any situation.

But it is especially true of bed-wetting, which is, after all, involuntary. A child does not deliberately wet the bed. S/he wakes up and discovers the linens and pajamas are soaked. Children in this situation are as bewildered—and often as distressed—as the adults around them. Most children are eager to please their parents, and feel puzzled and helpless when their bodies seem to be acting so unpredictably.

Studies have shown time and again that humiliating and punitive techniques are not only ineffective but downright counterproductive. The stress they create actually contributes to the problem. Responding to your child with warmth, love, and acceptance will be far more useful. More importantly, these attitudes will forge a stronger bond between you and your child, as you work together to deal with a situation that both of you want changed. You then function as your child's ally, rather than her/his adversary. Meeting a common challenge together can be an experience of growth, strength, and the joy of triumph.

EXPLORE PHYSICAL CAUSES

If bed-wetting has become a persistent problem, then your pediatrician should be your first port of call. There are a variety of organic conditions that may be behind it.

Your child may have a urinary tract infection or chronic cystitis. Food allergies are another common culprit. Sickle-cell anemia is among several illnesses that lead to enuresis. Once identified, they can be addressed, and the enuresis resolved.

Not all physical causes are serious or even disease-related. Your child may simply have a very small bladder. If this is the case, your doctor may recommend a regimen of exercises to expand the bladder capacity.

Some doctors recommend drugs to help stop bed-wetting. Their motive is not to heal a specific disease, but rather to put an end to an annoying problem. Unfortunately, many of these drugs have adverse side effects. Some might even create long-term health hazards. There are many other excellent means of dealing with bed-wetting without resorting to such measures.

TAKE NOTE OF YOUR CHILD'S SLEEPING PATTERNS

Some children wet their beds because they sleep very, very deeply. They are in such a profound state of sleep that they're unaware of their own bodily signals. They remain oblivious to the release of urine and even sleep through wet linens. They realize that they urinated only when they wake up in the morning.

Is your child a heavy sleeper? Can you talk, sing, bang a hammer, walk around, or open and close drawers in her/ his room and continue to hear snores coming from her/his bed? Can you touch, undress, or move her/him without interrupting those snores? If the answer to these questions is "yes," then you have an important clue to the bed-wetting.

Many parents find that waking their child and taking her/ him to the bathroom during the night (usually before they themselves go to sleep) is helpful. This way, the child doesn't need to depend on a bodily signal that will be missed due to sleep. Some parents notice that if a child is awakened night after night at approximately the same time, a pattern is established. The child's body will become accustomed to waking up at that hour and s/he will eventually wake up independently. Even if this doesn't happen in the long run, on a night-by-night basis, the child wakes up dry.

Some pediatricians, however, have raised questions about this practice. They point out that often the child isn't even fully awake when being taken to the bathroom. S/he's actually sleepwalking, or carried in parental arms and placed on the toilet, then carried back to bed. In other words, the child has urinated while asleep—except that s/he's done it in the toilet instead of in her bed. This has taught nothing about recognizing the urge to go while asleep, waking up, and using the toilet.

My own advice is, experiment and see what works! Some children are cranky and uncooperative upon being awakened during the night. If this is the case, then toileting becomes a battle, and the child might develop unpleasant associations with nighttime visits to the bathroom. But if your child is cooperative and willing to be led to the bathroom, and if this leads to a dry morning, then most parents feel it's worthwhile. Almost invariably, this is a transitional step to eventual dryness without being awakened during the night. (This is especially true if your child experiences nighttime incontinence because of a small bladder capacity. As s/he grows, the bladder grows, too, and makes it easier to retain urine until morning.)

There are mechanical devices available on the market that also address the heavy sleeper. These are moisture-sensitive pads connected to buzzers or alarms. When the pad begins to get wet, the alarm sounds, waking the child. The idea is to rouse the child from a deep sleep the moment urination starts.

At the beginning, the child probably won't wake up until s/he's finished and the bladder is completely empty. Gradually, however, s/he'll learn to associate urination with wakefulness. S/he may release a few drops, wake up, and finish the job in the toilet. The goal is to teach your child how to wake up when the bladder is full and the body is signaling a need to go.

Alarms boast a pretty high success rate—sometimes as high as 75 to 80 percent short-term effectiveness (within a few months). There are, however, some notable drawbacks. Some children actually sleep right through the alarm. The noise, however, might disrupt other family members—parents, siblings, pets. Some children who respond to the alarm wake up disturbed or upset. Perspiration can set off the buzzer, so its use diminishes considerably in the summertime. And many children regress once the alarm is removed.

Again, use your own intuition. Talk it over with your child. Explain how the buzzer works. (Many children are afraid of being electrocuted.) Some children are eager to try this new method, while others are reluctant. Don't be afraid to experiment and see what works. Be sure to read the instructions carefully. Many would-be successes have been thwarted by improper use of the device. Some companies lease the devices and offer counseling to ensure maximum effectiveness. Be guided by your own good sense and by the reactions of your child.

LIMIT BEDTIME FLUIDS

Many parents have found that limiting fluid intake at bedtime will curtail nighttime accidents. Of course, that does not mean cutting out all water, juice, or milk for the entire evening. Children, like adults, need fluids in their systems. Thirst is the body's way of signaling a physical need and should be responded to. But too much liquid before bed can overload the small bladder of a child.

CREATE A CONDUCIVE ENVIRONMENT

Children are more likely to urinate when they're cold. They're also going to be reluctant to get up during the night if this means getting out of a nice, cozy bed into a chilly room just to go to the bathroom. So try to keep your child's room warm and comfortable. Temperatures between 65 and 70 degrees Fahrenheit are perfect. The same applies to the bathroom and to any hallways between the bedroom and the bathroom.

Make sure your child's pajamas are warm and that there are plenty of blankets. It helps to keep slippers right by the bed, so that her/his feet are snug as well.

Some children are afraid of the dark and may not want to get up if the bathroom or hallways look dim or "spooky." So keep the hallway and bathroom well-lit and inviting.

Pajamas and underwear should be easy to remove. Some children are quite put off by complicated snaps or buttons or underwear that won't lower easily because it's too small. They may just decide that it's not worth the struggle and urinate in their beds instead.

EMOTIONAL CAUSES

Sometimes stress is at the root of a bed-wetting problem. Stress doesn't have to be caused by a "negative" circumstance: Sometimes the excitement of traveling, being in a new surrounding, anticipating a birthday or a visit from a grandparent, the birth of a new sibling, or the beginning of school can cause ripples in a child's equilibrium, resulting in a wet bed. Of course, illness, hospitalization, family friction, divorce, or a family death can also lead to nighttime accidents.

Sometimes sources of stress might not be so obvious. Your child might be reacting to a frightening movie, an overbearing teacher, or a menacing class bully. Parents have occasionally been alerted to cases of physical, sexual, or emotional abuse in a day-care center or school when their children suddenly started to wet their beds.

If you have, together with your pediatrician, ruled out physical causes, then it's time to explore emotional ones. The best way to begin is by talking to your child calmly, lovingly, and matter-of-factly. Reassure Alice that she is not alone, that many children deal with bed-wetting. Be positive and encouraging about her prospects of overcoming it. And in a loving, non-accusatory fashion, try to question her as to *why* she's wetting the bed. If she can't come up with an immediate explanation (such as "the house is dark and scary at night and I'm afraid to get up"), then try to gently probe further. It may take a few conversations, so don't be impatient. Children (and adults) don't like to be rushed and are more reluctant to open up if they feel someone's dragging information out of them. If your child seems unwilling to talk, don't press. Children are entitled to their privacy, and your prying might cause needless resentment. Reassure her of your love and willingness to be there for her, and drop the subject for a few days.

Don't ever assume that you "know" better than your child what's bothering him ("Oh, it's because of the new baby, isn't it?"). Even if you have a hunch that Mike's jealous of the new arrival, you really don't *know* what's going on in his head. He may be upset about something else. He may be excited by all the guests in and out of the house. He may not like having his uncle, who's helping with the baby, sleeping in his room. Always remain open to what he has to say, and try to get *him* to tell *you* what's on his mind.

Some children aren't talkers. You ask them a question and they shrug, or mumble, "I d'know." For them, a game like 20 questions might work nicely ("Is it that you're jealous of the new baby? Are you cold when you get out of bed? Do you like your teacher?"). Some children will express more freely through drawing, clay, or doll play. Careful observation and listening might give you the clue you need.

If you suspect that your child is wetting because s/he is experiencing some stress, then address the problem at its root, by dealing with the stressful situation, rather than simply addressing the symptom. Become a detective and talk to teachers, day-care providers, and others who are in contact with her/him. Once you have identified the problem, you can handle it appropriately and, in most cases, the enuresis will disappear. (If it lingers, even once the stress has been removed, then use some of the other techniques outlined here.)

If you are unable to identify a source of stress, or are having difficulty helping your child deal with whatever is bothering her/him, then seek professional counseling from a competent counselor.

TRY TO KEEP SIBLINGS FROM TEASING

Since stress or poor self-image are so often linked with bed-wetting, it's especially important to keep siblings (and classmates, as the case might be) from teasing your child. When speaking to these other children, don't be harsh, accusatory, or angry. This simply creates resentment, which almost invariably will be directed at your child. Rather, explain in a kind, friendly tone that Seth is already having a difficult time, that he can't control his nighttime urination, and that, like anybody else with a physical difficulty, he needs support and understanding.

HAVE YOUR CHILD ASSUME RESPONSIBILITY FOR CLEANUP

Responsibility is very different from blame. While a child shouldn't be blamed for bed-wetting, s/he should be encouraged to take responsibility for it and to assist in cleanup. Children can be taught to strip their beds, change their own clothes, and carry their wet stuff to the sink, tub, or washroom. If you know your child wets regularly, then double-sheet the bed. You can make the bed with layers: first, a rubber mattress cover, then a sheet, then a second rubber cover, then a second sheet. Your child can remove the top two layers and crawl right back into bed. Depending on her/his age, s/he might not even need to wake you at all!

There are a number of advantages to this, not least of which, you'll get extra sleep—no small matter, when you have to be up early to take care of kids the next morning! More importantly, this removes any secondary gain your child might be getting from the wetting. (Being the center of attention at a time when the rest of the house is sleeping can be very attractive to a child.) The less you are involved, the less your child commands your attention as a result of an undesirable behavior. Lastly, your child learns that, while bed-wetting is not her/his fault, it *is* her/his responsibility, and that it's not fair to expect Mommy or Daddy to clean up the mess.

PRESLEEP SUGGESTIONS

Children are especially receptive to suggestions whispered into their ears just as they're falling asleep. There are tapes available on the market that are written for the purpose. One tape contains a bedtime story and a guidebook for parents. Other tapes are subliminally oriented, designed to address the child's unconscious mind.

You can design your own tape and play it to your son as he's falling asleep, or even in his sleep. Or you can simply talk to him. Tell him how much you love him. Tell him how wonderful he is, how you *know* he can stay dry, wake up dry, and how proud you are. If you wake him up to take him to the bathroom, whisper these things in his ear as you guide him through the steps. The more loved he feels, the more secure he'll be, and the less stressed.

VISUALIZATION

Visualization—creating mental images of desired goals—has become a popular tool in dealing with medical as well as emotional problems. It works quite well with bed-wetting.

Ask Stevie to lie down or sit comfortably with his eyes closed. You can do this throughout the day, but it's especially effective at bedtime. Ask him to describe a relaxing or enjoyable activity or scene and encourage him to see this as his "safe" place, always there for him to relax. Ask him to picture himself waking up dry, feeling proud and good. Again, reassure him of your love, your confidence in him, and in his ability to remain dry.

STAR CHARTS AND OTHER REWARDS

Some children respond well to the promise of a reward (a small toy, a special trip, extra time with Mom or Dad) if they can stay dry for a certain number of days—say, a week. A star chart is an excellent way to provide daily encouragement (most children are interested and pleased watching those bright stars accumulating on the chart) and mark the dry days. Each time Mary wakes up dry, she gets a star. She doesn't, however, get penalized for wet mornings by having a star removed. She simply doesn't get a star for that day. After receiving a certain number of stars (a smaller number for a younger child, a larger number for an older child), she gets an agreed-upon reward.

Bed-wetting is a challenging situation. The key: Remain calm, loving, and positive. And be an optimist—your child will almost certainly outgrow it, and will do so even more quickly if you help her/him along the way!

SUGGESTIONS FOR FURTHER READING

Scharf, Martin B. *Waking Up Dry: How to End Bedwetting Forever*. Cincinnati: Writer's Digest Books, 1986.

Schaeffer, Charles. *Childhood Enuresis and Encopresis*. New York: Van Nostrand Reinhold and Co, 1979.

11

Encopresis (Fecal Soiling)

Chapter 10 discussed bed-wetting as a fairly common phenomenon among school-age children. Despite its frequent occurrence, parents and children continue to feel embarrassment when bed-wetting occurs. The shame they feel is compounded by their sense of isolation. They don't talk about their problem because they're too embarrassed; and because nobody talks about the problem, the children don't realize that other children are dealing with it as well.

If this is true of enuresis, it's doubly and triply true of encopresis. Children who continue to soil their underwear beyond their toddler years are even more isolated and ashamed than children who wet their beds. You can walk through supermarkets or libraries and scan the bulletin boards, or turn on the television and find advertisements for buzzer systems to help bed-wetters. Not so for soilers. Encopresis is the Big Taboo. Parents, teachers, peers, and even professionals often react with disgust and revulsion at the odor of feces (especially in an older child) and the very notion that a school-age child could be producing bowel movements anywhere but the bathroom. As mentioned in Chapter 1, problems experienced in toilet training are among the leading causes of child abuse in this country.

This is greatly compounded when the child is out of her/his toddler years and "should know better."

ATTITUDE

"Attitude again?" you ask as you prepare to read this chapter. "Can't a chapter go by without some reference to attitude?"

No. Attitude is central to each chapter, but especially those chapters dealing with children who are experiencing special problems or difficult situations. These are the circumstances under which many parents feel irritated or imposed upon, ashamed of their children, or overwhelmed by them. These are times in which parental anger can worsen an already difficult situation and can even lead to severe child abuse if not handled correctly.

Encopresis rarely happens deliberately. A variety of physical or psychological reasons may be responsible for your child's soiling. Most of the time, your child will be as eager as you are to end this problem and lead a life like other "normal" children.

If you find yourself angry, ashamed, or disappointed in your child, reread Chapter 1, "Attitude." It will help you deal with the situation effectively and learn to handle your child's soiling without damaging your relationship with her/him. In fact, you and your child can emerge stronger allies than ever before.

A VISIT TO YOUR DOCTOR

Soiling often occurs because of a physiological problem. There are a number of physical reasons why children suffer from encopresis.

Hirschsprung's disease (also known as congenital megacolon) is an illness that robs children of the normal sensations informing them of a full bowel, as well as the normal peristaltic waves that move feces through the intestines and out of the body. If your child receives a diagnosis of Hirschsprung's disease, your doctor will probably seek to correct it surgically. For a discussion of problems that may arise in toilet training after surgery, see Chapter 12, "Special Situations."

A second physiological cause for soiling is anatomic megacolon. This occurs when lesions or tumors obstruct the bowel. Ulcerative colitis can occasionally lead to fecal incontinence as well. Your doctor will determine which of these illnesses, if any, affect your child, and will recommend a course of treatment that may include change in diet, visualization and biofeedback, medication, or surgery.

Your doctor may also discover that your child's diet is deficient in fiber and is overloaded with dairy, junk foods, and other items that may have an impact on the digestive system. Allergies will also be explored because they sometimes contribute to bowel problems.

It's important to prepare your child for the medical examination ahead of time. Inform yourself in advance what procedures might be required, and share this information with your child. Children are as sensitive to issues of privacy as adults, and many of the diagnostic procedures invade parts of the body that the child already recognizes as private. Some procedures also involve pain. Without scaring your child, discuss these things before they actually take place. Try to find out whether your presence in the room during the examination or procedure would be appreciated by your child, or whether it would be resented. Some children feel comforted and secure when their parents stay in the room during a medical procedure. Others prefer their privacy. Let your child guide you, and indicate your willingness to be supportive in whatever way s/he feels best.

If surgery is required, there are several steps you can take to make the experience easier:

1) Prepare your child ahead of time about what to expect.

2) There are some excellent books available for different age groups on the subject of a trip to the hospital and an operation.

3) Many children play out their fears and concerns using drawings, clay, dolls, or other toys. (This is the case even with older children.) Try to have these items readily available, and don't tell your older child that s/he's "too big to play with dolls."

4) Respect your child's privacy. don't talk about her/him and her/his personal bodily functions to family members if s/he's sensitive about these things. If solicitous friends and family members would like updates, then fill them in on the desired information in your child's absence.

5) Treat your child with dignity. Allow Alan to answer as many questions about his own body as possible, instead of rushing in and saying "he has four bowel movements a day." Never conduct conversations about his condition as if he weren't in the room. Either include him in the discussion, or conduct it privately.

6) While it's important to relax pressure at this time, don't throw all your household rules out the window. Many parents feel so sorry for their sick children that they overcompensate by allowing all sorts of breaches of family rules that they would never tolerate from their other children. Your child needs to feel your firmness and consistency as much as ever.

7) If your child feels embarrassed about her/his condition, explore her/his beliefs about these things. You might consider seeking a self-help group or some professional counseling.

8) Be reassuring and as happy as you can be. Your child needs your love and your inner peace, not your feelings of guilt, sorrow, or pity.

THE NEVER-BEEN-TRAINED CHILD

A common cause of encopresis in older children is the neglect to teach them otherwise. Sometimes parents who adopt the laissez-faire attitude mentioned in Chapter 4, Approaches to Toilet Training, simply wait and wait for their child to "catch on" independently—and it never happens.

Some parents just don't get around to toilet training. Perhaps there's a stressful life situation going on—a divorce, a prolonged illness, a disruptive business schedule—and the parents keep putting it off until they turn around and discover that their five-year-old is still wearing diapers.

Whatever the reason, if your child is still soiling because you haven't really taken toilet training in hand, don't blame yourself. Your feelings of guilt will not help you or your child. Concentrate instead on how you can remedy the situation now.

Begin by explaining to your child that it's time for her/him to learn how to use the potty. As much as possible, be frank and say that you think you've made a mistake in not bringing this up sooner. Discuss your reasoning candidly and your decision to work together with your child at bringing about a change. Your child will probably respect your honesty. Then continue with the steps outlined in Chapter 8, "Toilet Training the Older Child."

CONSTIPATION

Constipation is one of the most common reasons for encopresis. It sounds paradoxical, to be sure, because soiling seems like the inability to hold bowel movements in rather

than the inability to get them out. But constipation can lead
to soiling. Here's how.

A constipated child often develops an impacted rectum.
Feces build up and harden, distending the rectum. The rectal muscles lose their elasticity and become stretched out.
They become unable to respond to the presence of feces.
Thus the child no longer experiences the sensation of fullness and internal signal to defecate. The stools continue to
build up.

The rectal wall also begins to lose its capacity to absorb
water, so some liquidy stools leak out from behind the impacted feces. The child is usually unaware of the passage
of this liquid and is surprised—and usually distressed—to
discover her/his soiled underwear.

Chronic constipation can occur as a result of several reasons, many of which we touched on in Chapter 9, "General
Tips," section on constipation:

1) Fear, stress, or emotional turmoil may lead to constipation in many children. If you think this might be the case
with your child, then try to address the causes with her/
him. Ask yourself, too, whether you might have contributed
to this stress by being too domineering and controlling, especially regarding toileting matters. If you draw a blank,
then consider consulting a professional counselor.

2) Scheduling problems. Some children wake up five
minutes before the school bus comes, throw on their
clothes, and rush out of the house, barely getting to the bus
on time. They are so concerned about not being late that
they are unable to take the time they need in the bathroom.
Others are fine in the morning, but ignore Nature's call after
school when they're busy playing, doing homework, or being engaged in other activities, from which they're unwilling to tear themselves away to use the bathroom. Still
others are constantly being hurried out of the bathroom by

household members who'd like to get in.

If you think your child might be constipated because of one of these reasons, then sit down and discuss it together. Plan out a strategy. Perhaps s/he'll need to go to bed 15 minutes earlier, and set the alarm clock 15 minutes earlier, so as to have sufficient time in the morning before the school bus arrives. Perhaps it would help to set up a household rule that your child can't watch TV after school, or go outside to play until s/he's visited the bathroom first. Perhaps you can work out a family bathroom plan that will remove some of the pressure from your child and allow her/him to finish her/his business in a relaxed and unhurried way.

3) Diet: We discussed diet at great length in Chapter 9, ''General Tips,'' section on Constipation. If your child is constipated, examine her/his diet and make any necessary alterations—perhaps in consulation with your doctor or a nutritionist.

4) Exercise stimulates the digestive system and is an excellent way to get the bowels moving.

5) A soothing warm bath and some gentle massage of the abdominal area might also help. Bathing in a tub filled with chamomile tea (use six to seven tea bags, per tubful of water) relaxes the internal muscles and may allow the stool to pass.

6) If all of the above fail, then consult Dr. Charles E. Schaeffer's book *Childhood Encopresis and Enuresis: Causes and Therapy* for a course of treatment, involving enemas, laxatives, and possibly some medication as well. Discuss any treatment program with your doctor before proceeding.

7) Offer a reward for proper toileting. You can use a star chart (your child receives a star or sticker for each clean day, and receives a prize after earning a certain agreed-upon number of stars), or have a bowl of small prizes handy right

in the bathroom for every time s/he uses the toilet or potty correctly.

8) It is important to help your child accept responsibility for cleanup as well. This is, as mentioned earlier, not punitive. You don't need to be angry or judgmental toward your child. It's merely teaching her/him to assume responsibility for cleaning up her/his own mess. This is an important part of growing up. Plus, it may serve as a strong deterrent for future soiling. If Kevin is aware that he'll have to wash out his own soiled underwear, he'll probably feel additionally motivated to participate in a program that may be painful (releasing impacted stool can be quite painful), time-consuming (at least at first), and potentially embarrassing.

9) Try to keep siblings and other children from teasing. Nasty remarks won't help your child to stay clean. They'll only contribute to her/his feeling even worse. If your child's siblings are ashamed of their sister/brother's problem, then address the matter with them lovingly and nonjudgmentally. Don't be afraid to share your own feelings, if you've experienced similar emotions. Your children will probably respect you more and will be more likely to learn to deal with their own emotions if you're open about yours. Explain that you're dealing with the problem and that you hope it'll be resolved soon.

If you handle encopresis calmly and lovingly, chances are that you'll be able to put this difficult phase behind you pretty quickly. Once it's over, keep an eye on your child's bathroom schedule, eating and exercise habits, and stress levels to make sure s/he's not falling back into patterns that have had a deleterious effect on her/his digestive system.

REFERENCES AND SUGGESTIONS FOR FUTURE READING

Schaeffer, Charles and DiGeronimo, Theresa Foy. *Toilet Training Without Tears.* New York: Signet Books, 1989.

Schaeffer, Charles E. *Childhood Enuresis and Encopresis.* New York: Van Nostrand Reinhold and Co., 1979.

12

Special Situations

There are many children in special situations whose needs are often not addressed by general books. This seems to be the case especially with toilet training. Often agencies, organizations, and self-help groups that are designed to provide information to parents seem to draw blanks when it comes to toilet training issues.

This chapter is not an exhaustive and extensive treatise on toilet training children with special needs. It is designed to start you off, make some suggestions and observations about special children in general and toilet training in particular. Several resources that can offer you more help are listed at the end of the chapter.

TWINS, TRIPLETS, AND MORE

Parents of twins can attest to the fact that they have their hands quite full! (This goes triply for triplets, and increases with the number of children.) Somehow, it seems more complicated than simply multiplying one times two. The work brought on by twins is an exponential multiple of the work required by a single child. So are the rewards.

1) *When to begin.* Many parents of twins start toilet training later than parents of non-twins. Perhaps this is because they feel that they already have so much work, they're reluctant to take on a new responsibility. There is, however, no intrinsic reason why twins can't learn toileting as early as any other child.

2) *Equipment you'll need.* It is advisable to buy each child her/his own potty. There are several practical reasons for this. One is that your children are less likely to fight if they each have their own potty. The second is that they may both have to use the potty at the same time.

Some child-care experts suggest buying each twin a different style of potty. They feel that this enhances the twins' sense of individuality, and makes it easy for each to know which is "mine." Others feel that this isn't necessary. On the contrary, they may both end up fighting over the blue potty, even though the yellow one is just as good. (Of course, you can resolve that by insisting that they take turns with both potties.) As with so many other aspects of parenting, there are no hard-and-fast rules. You know your children best. Follow your instincts.

Twins will also need double the number of training pants. Here, too, it's a matter of individual choice if you buy two dozen identical pants or different designs for each child.

If you are using the design on the pants as a motivator for speedier training, however, then the particular design might make a difference. One twin may like Sesame Street characters, while the other may prefer pictures of animals. Guide yourself by their own unique tastes.

3) *Readiness.* Be aware that all twins—even identical— are unique individuals. Billy may not be ready for the potty until he's three, while Bobby might be trained by the time he's two. This is quite normal. Don't hold one twin back, and don't pressure the other. Let each proceed at his own pace.

4) *Praise.* Some parents are reluctant to praise one twin in the presence of the other. If Susie uses the potty but Sally refuses, they feel that praising Susie will lead to jealous feelings in Sally. They wonder if Sally's self-esteem may not suffer.

If praise is delivered tactfully, however, this needn't happen. There's no reason why Susie should be deprived of praise just because Sally isn't receiving any. What's important is that you confine your praise to Susie's accomplishments, rather than making an invidious comparison between Susie and Sally. It's better not to say something like "Susie is so much quicker than Sally. Look how nicely she made in the potty!" Concentrate instead on praising Susie as a person in her own right. "Susie, I'm so proud that you used the potty!"

5) *Rewards.* Rewarding one twin and not the other raises the same issue as praising one twin and not the other. If you feel you'd like to reward Johnny for using the potty, then do so without putting down Jennie and without withdrawing any of Jennie's privileges. Make sure you find plenty of other opportunities in the course of the day to praise and reward Jennie as well.

Remember that watching you praise and reward the successful twin might provide an additional incentive for the slower twin to follow suit.

GIGGLE MICTURITION (ALSO KNOWN AS GIGGLE URINATION)

A small number of children experience the inability to contain their urine when they are laughing. This is called Giggle Micturition (or Giggle Urination).

Certainly don't deal with this challenge by eliminating

laughter from your child's life! There are several effective approaches you can take.

1) Assure your child that there are other children who face this challenge. Call it a "challenge" rather than a "problem."

2) Speak to your doctor to make sure there are no medical reasons for this. Perhaps s/he will recommend a series of exercises to strengthen the bladder muscles.

3) Children are notorious for waiting until the last minute to use the bathroom, because they're too busy doing other things. Your child can't afford to do this. Set up a bathroom schedule together (say, every hour) so that your child's bladder is never close to full capacity.

When you're setting up a bathroom schedule, make sure that you don't become the resident nag. At the beginning, it's fine to give your child hourly reminders. Encourage schoolteachers, camp counselors, and group leaders to do the same. But as your child gets older, these reminders may become embarrassing. S/he must learn to become autonomous. So buy your child a watch and encourage her/him to consult it regularly. Today, many watches have a built-in alarm feature and can be set to beep or play a melody at a particular time. This might be both useful and entertaining for your child in keeping track of the bathroom schedule.

4) Encourage your child to visit the bathroom before being in a setting in which there's likely to be a lot of laughter and fun—a comedy movie, an amusement park, getting together with a group of friends, sitting at your family dinner table, if that's a time of shared laughter.

5) Some adults love to tickle and roughhouse with children. In fact, they don't know how to entertain children in any other way. For most kids, this is great fun. But a child with weak bladder control often finds rough play and tickling to be a nightmare.

So discuss your child's bladder with anyone who has your kids shrieking with hysterical laughter as s/he chases them around the room. Mention it to teachers and others who will be with your child for long periods of time. And work with your child at the same time on learning assertiveness with adults if s/he doesn't want to be touched or played with in a particular way. (This is a good idea to do with children anyway.) Ultimately, your child will probably outgrow the problem or will learn effective ways to handle it independently.

6) If these methods fail, then consult a clinic that specializes in problems of enuresis.

LEAKS

Some children who are fully toilet trained nevertheless dribble out small quantities of urine into their underwear. Some have frequent daytime accidents as well. (This is not to be confused with children who, in a frightening or stressful situation, have an accident.) These children often have a small bladder capacity, and as their bodies grow, their bladders will grow with them and they will leave the problem behind.

Some children leak because their bladder doesn't fully empty. They are in too much of a hurry when they use the bathroom and don't allow the last drops to come out. (This seems to be a little more common in girls.) So encourage your child to relax and not to rush the process. You might suggest to your child to count to ten when at the end just to make sure there's ample time for any remaining urine to come out.

For some children, the difficulty lies in muscular coordination. They can't seem to coordinate their need to urinate with their sphincter and pelvic floor muscles. For these children, a very effective method called urodynamic biofeedback has been developed. After careful study and measurement of the child's urinary patterns, the child learns to "read" what's happening within her/his bladder by being attached to a biofeedback machine and watching a visual representation on a graph. The electrodes measure bladder fullness and muscle activity. The doctors then teach the child how to relax and contract the bladder muscles, and by watching the screen, the child immediately sees whether s/he's doing it right.

This method is still rather new and may be hard to come by, so you might have to do some legwork to track it down if you think it would be helpful to your child. Some suggestions follow in the Resources section at the end of this chapter.

As with other urinary problems, stress is always a factor that should be considered. When a child feels tense, the bladder is a common target organ. Bladder walls may become thickened and irritated. This can happen due to lack of sufficient exercise; it can also happen as a result of too much stress. Investigate possible causes of stress with your child. Consider having your child talk to an outsider—perhaps a warm and loving grandparent, neighbor, or friend, or a professional counselor.

Some doctors will prescribe drugs to control wetting. (See Chapter 10 for a more complete discussion.) If at all possible, try to work out a different solution because the drugs often have side effects that are worse than the problem itself.

CHILDREN WITH HANDICAPS—GENERAL REMARKS

Having a child with a special health situation is a unique challenge for most parents. On the one hand, they don't want to push their child and demand activities that may be beyond the child's physical or psychological capabilities. A child with no legs can't become an Olympic runner no matter how hard you push.

On the other hand, it can be equally problematic to set expectations that are too low. If you believe your child to be incapable of a skill or task, s/he will probably live up to those expectations. This is called a self-fulfilling prophecy. Limiting beliefs like these rob your child of the opportunity to fulfill her/his potential.

In her book *A Circle of Children,* learning specialist Mary MacCracken describes her work with severely emotionally disturbed children. She describes how she toilet trained a group of children who were believed by others to be untrainable. Her goals were to teach them to take care of their own bodily needs—eat, dress themselves, and use the bathroom.

"Zoe [a fellow worker who had more experience with these children] told me later how impossible my goals were—but because I was new, alone in my room at the far end of the hall, and had no one to tell me otherwise, I did not know it." MacCracken achieved her goals with all but one child.

1) *Finding a balance.* Remember that while toileting is important, it isn't everything. As important as it is for a child (and an adult) to be able to take care of her/himself in this personal area of her/his life, and to achieve maximum independence in all areas, it's equally important for there to be quality of life. If it's going to take your child several hours to toilet her/himself independently, while an aide could accomplish the task within minutes, then it's important to discuss with your child what the priorities are here.

Ultimately, the toileting decision will be your child's. Strive to help her/him reach maximum independence, but continue to remain open to alternatives. Above all, help her/

him reach a decision that will be best for *her/him*, not for you or anyone else.

2) *Focus on your child's strengths.* Toilet learning involves several different skills: motor (the ability to walk to the potty, sit down, release the wastes, and so on); and cognitive (the ability to understand what's required—that waste belongs in the potty, not in a diaper, underwear, or on the floor).

If your child has a deficit in some area of her/his body or development, then focus on her/his strengths in other areas. A child with motor delays may be able to understand the concepts involved in toileting long before s/he is actually capable of carrying out the necessary steps. A mentally retarded child, on the other hand, will learn more effectively by going through the process and being rewarded, rather than listening to lengthy explanations or reading books about toileting.

3) *Be patient.* Children with special needs often master toileting skills later than other children. It doesn't have to be this way—as we will see when we examine individual situations; quite a few special children achieve toilet mastery at the same time as their nonhandicapped counterparts. But if your child is delayed in this area, don't worry. It's quite normal. It doesn't mean that she will remain in diapers for life.

4) *Don't use coercion.* A handicapped child has a right to as much respect and dignity as any other child. Strapping a child to a potty, threatening, or hitting are cruel and ineffective ways to train a child, no matter what the child's circumstances are. In fact, a staff member at the Option Institute and Fellowship told me that most of the toilet training problems she has observed in the special children who have attended Institute programs have come about as a result of excessively harsh and coercive training. Instead, make the process fun! Invite your child to join in, don't command her/him like an army general. It will be more effective and will also help build a loving and trusting relationship between you and your child.

5) *Adaptive equipment.* Acquaint yourself with any adaptive toilet equipment that might be necessary or helpful to your child. There are devices that can be attached to a toilet to enable children with particular motor difficulties to use it effectively. Support bars can be installed in your bathroom. Make sure these items are in place before you start the training process so that they can be incorporated into your child's routine.

6) *Trust yourself and your child.* While professionals—doctors, nurses, teachers, social workers, and other helping professionals—are often helpful resources in dealing with a special child, *you* the parents are your child's best resource. Allow your own intuitions and awarenesses to guide you through toilet training, just as you do in other aspects of parenting.

It's important to trust your child as well, allowing her/him to set the pace and guide you through the process. If you follow your child's cues, you motivate your child to explore and develop.

BLIND CHILDREN

Blind or visually impaired children are often delayed in their toilet training skills. There are several reasons for this. One is that they can't actually see other people (or dolls) using the potty. The other is that language or motor delays often accompany blindness. Therefore you might want to start somewhat later than you would with a sighted child because you will rely more heavily upon language to explain to the child what's going on and what is expected of her/him.

1) Allow your child to explore the bathroom. Name all the fixtures, and explain what they're for. Allow and encourage touching.

2) Allow your child to familiarize her/himself with the potty before initiating its use.

3) Always keep the potty in the same place in the bathroom. If, for some reason, the potty must be moved, make sure you tell your child and guide her/him to the new location.

4) Make sure the bathroom floor is clear and free of bathtub toys, slippery mats, or other items over which your child could fall.

5) Keep the way to the bathroom clear and free of obstacles.

6) Since blind children rely more heavily than sighted children on their sense of smell, it would help if your bathroom smelled attractive. You can use scented soap or a potpourri dish to enhance the aroma.

7) Allow your child to accompany you to the bathroom and give a running commentary about what you're doing and why. Blind children do not receive the subtle visual cues that sighted children receive. They need your verbal explanations as to what's happening.

8) Teach your child to feel around the rim of the toilet or potty so as to make sure that the toilet paper gets dropped inside, rather than on the floor.

9) Orient your child to other bathrooms in frequently visited places (school, Grandma's house, and so on).

10) Blind boys *can* be taught to urinate in a standing position. Teach them to place their feet at the base of the toilet and listen for the splash of the water so as to ascertain whether they've aimed correctly. If they discover that they've sprinkled the seat or the floor, teach them how to clean up after themselves.

11) Be clear and consistent in your terminology, and acquaint your child with the various body parts, their names and functions.

DEAF CHILDREN

In the case of deaf children, you will obviously be relying on their vision to convey to them what you want them to know about toilet training.

1) It is extremely important to allow them to watch you or others on the toilet. Books with pictures about toileting are also useful.

2) Depending on your child's age and level of verbal understanding, you probably won't want to engage in explanations as to what's happening. Instead, choose a single word and sign and verbalize it whenever you use the toilet.

3) After your child has become accustomed to seeing you use the toilet, place her/him on the potty. Verbalize and sign the word you've been using.

4) Be consistent. Don't call it a "tinkle" sometimes and a "pee-pee" other times. Your child might become confused.

5) Praise (and, if you like, reward) any production, repeating the signed word.

6) You may wish to start training your deaf child later than you would train hearing children, because an older child has probably established better communication with you. One parent of a deaf girl told me that her communication with her daughter was excellent. The parents had started learning sign language when their daughter was a baby, and she herself was signing fluently by the time she was three. Therefore toilet training her was no different from toilet training her older brothers, who were not deaf.

CHILDREN WHO ARE BLIND AND DEAF

Children who are blind and deaf lack both the visual and the auditory cues that are available to other children. Therefore the training process must be somewhat modified to maximize their cognitive and motor abilities.

1) Remove your child's diapers and put her/him in training pants, at least during the day. A plastic shell can be used to protect your floor. The idea is to accustom your child to the feeling of wet and dry underwear, which is almost impossible in today's sophisticated, ultra-absorbent diapers. You also want your child to develop a preference for dry underwear.

2) Help your child to feel her/his pants. If they are wet, say and sign the word for *wet*. (You can heighten her/his awareness of wet and dry by introducing her/him to other wet items, each time signing and saying the word *wet*.)

3) Take your child to the bathroom if you discover wet pants. You want her/him to learn that wet pants belong in the bathroom.

4) Change your child's pants, and encourage her/him to help you do so. As your child gets older, you'll teach her/him how to do so independently.

5) When your child is wearing dry pants, help her/him feel them. Say and sign the word *dry*. Be lavish in your praise, and be sure to convey that you like dry pants.

6) Keep aware of your child's bowel patterns and visit the bathroom at the anticipated times. Punctuate the day with regular visits so as to make sure that there are ample opportunities for urination into the potty as well. When it's time for her/him to go, then call her/him by name. Use her/

his name sign. Then make the sign for *toilet*. Teach your child the sign as well.

7) When your child has urinated into the potty, make the sign for *wet* and point to the urine. Make the sign for *dry* and point to her/his underwear. Be lavish in your praise of her/his dryness, with lots of hugs and kisses. A small treat will reinforce your pleasure in her/his behavior.

8) If your child wets outside the bathroom, make the sign for *wet*. Take her/him to the bathroom and make the sign for *toilet*. Make sure s/he helps you change the wet clothing her/himself.

9) Your child will gradually begin to recognize the sign and associate it with the desired behavior.

10) Make sure everyone in your child's life is using the same word and sign. It may help to put up a poster in the bathroom with a picture of the word and the sign used.

11) The world may seem like a bewildering place for a child who can neither see nor hear. Routine is comforting to all children, especially children in this situation. Always use the same routine, the same word, and the same sign. This will help build feelings of security and trust.

12) Don't flush the toilet while the child is sitting on it. You may think that because your child can't hear, s/he won't be scared by the noise. But your child *can* feel the vibrations and can feel the water suddenly spraying her/his bottom. As your child becomes accustomed to the bathroom, you can teach flushing.

13) Don't leave her/him alone in the bathroom, especially at first. Little by little you'll be able to move farther away, as your child becomes more accustomed to the bathroom.

14) Use easy-to-manage clothing. Ultimately, you'll want your child to be able to pull her/his own pants up and down without assistance.

AUTISTIC CHILDREN

The autistic child is a riddle in many ways. Often so beautiful physically, there seems to be some neurological miswiring that leads these children to lock themselves in a self-stimulating universe that exludes those who love them. Some autistic children are also mentally retarded; most, however, are not. Many are highly intelligent, even brilliant, but lack the ability to manifest their intelligence in a societally acceptable way.

1) Be loving and accepting of your child. Books written by adults who were once autistic children show again and again that autistic children are often acutely aware of disapproval, disappointment, and anger in the people around them, even though they may not show that they notice or care.

2) Don't try to touch or force your child if s/he resists.

3) Try to assess your child's strength and use them. One special-education teacher had an autistic girl in her class who was obsessed with numbers. The teacher made up a series of numbered picture cards showing the various steps involved in using the toilet (walking to the bathroom, opening the door, pulling down her pants, sitting on the potty, and so on). The little girl was trained very quickly.

4) Make the process as interesting and inviting as possible.

5) Food rewards can be quite effective.

6) Most autistic children prefer routine and sameness, so keep a neat, sweet-smelling, well-organized bathroom, and incorporate a regular pottying schedule into your day.

CHILDREN WITH OSTOMIES

An ostomy is a surgical opening in the abdominal wall through which waste is discharged. It can be internal or external, permanent or temporary. A urostomy takes care of the emptying of urine; an ileostomy or colostomy is used for removal of feces.

Children receive ostomies for a number of different reasons. Hirschprung's disease, Crohn's disease, Imperforate Anus, Vater's Syndrome, and ulcerative colitis are some examples of illnesses that may necessitate ileostomies or colostomies. There are several birth defects, cancer, or traumas that can necessitate ostomies as well.

1) Throughout this book, I recommend conducting bowel and bladder training together for most children. If your child has an ostomy, however, this might not be possible. A child with a colostomy may be capable of being bladder trained by age two-and-a-half, but it may take several more years before s/he is ready to empty her ostomy device her/himself. A child with a urostomy can be bowel trained at the same time as other children, but will need some special training in learning to empty her/his own device.

So proceed with training the unaffected part of the child as you would with any other child. You may need to do some extra explaining (''Your pee-pee works just like Dad's, but your poops come out differently).''

2) While your child may not be completed with training for a while, it's a good idea to begin somewhere between two and three years old. Be prepared for a long process, and don't be discouraged by other children who toilet train more quickly.

3) Since most ostomy children don't have the opportunity to observe others with ostomies, it's helpful to show them what to do by using a doll. The idea isn't necessarily to get an anatomically correct doll with its own ostomy, but to attach the appliance to any doll, explain what to do, and let your child learn to change the doll's pouch.

4) Teaching a child with an ostomy to tend to her/his own device will come in two phases: One is teaching her/him to empty the appliance; the other is teaching her/him to change it. It will take longer to learn how to change it than how to empty it.

5) It's easier for children to learn to empty urostomies than it is to empty ileostomies or colostomies because all they have to do is let the urine out through the tip of the appliance, through a device that's like a little spigot. It's easy to handle and not messy.

6) Let your child do as much as possible her/himself, even before s/he's ready to handle it all independently.

7) When your child goes to preschool or kindergarten, talk to her/his teacher ahead of time. Explain that when your child asks to use the bathroom, s/he *really* needs to go and should always be allowed to do so. Educate the teachers about her/his physical condition. Some children will continue to need help in the bathroom or regular reminders to go, even in preschool. In most states, children are entitled to receive such help from a teacher, aide, or school nurse. Don't be shy to ask for it! You might arrange a signal between teacher and student so your child can alert the teacher of the need to go without being too conspicuous.

8) Set up a bathroom schedule with your child. Children with ostomies lack the sensation of "needing to go to the bathroom." Urine or feces flow into their appliances on a steady basis. They may begin to recognize when their appliances become heavy but, being children, will probably wait until the last minute to empty or change the pouch.

Encourage them to be regular, and give them a watch to help them. Some children are reluctant to use the public bathroom due to the lack of privacy. If this is the case, you can probably arrange for your child to use the nurse's office or teacher's lounge bathroom.

9) Try to network with other parents of ostomy children. They often have practical suggestions, born out of the wisdom of experience. See if your children can meet their children. Kids with ostomies often feel that they're the only ones who have this "crazy" way of excreting. It can be comforting to know that there are others in the same boat as well.

10) Children who've had ostomies that were later reversed need to learn to excrete in a normal way as part of their toilet training. This can be a difficult process and needs professional guidance. Consult the resources at the end of this chapter as to how to find a program that teaches the child to recognize and respond to ordinary excretory signals. Reassure your child that inability to control excreta is not a failure but the result of illness, and encourage patience and self-acceptance.

CHILDREN WITH SPINA BIFIDA

Spina bifida is the incomplete formation of the spinal column. The normal closure of the column does not take place, and the nerves grow outward, forming a meningomyelocele. Nerve connections needed for walking, bowel and bladder control may be interrupted.

1) Children with spina bifida lack the sensations that alert other children to the need to go. Most cannot achieve bladder control. Urine must be removed from their bodies regularly through intermittent catheterization. When your child is young, you the parents, the school nurse, or an aide

will need to assist your child. But as your child grows, s/he can be taught to catheterize independently. Much will depend on your child's level of maturity and degree of motor coordination.

2) Because the nerves controlling the rectal sphincter muscle are usually affected as well, your child will not experience rectal fullness. S/he can be taught, however, to visit the bathroom on a scheduled basis. If meals are regular, bowel movements will probably be regular as well, so a schedule shouldn't be too difficult to set up.

3) Children with spina bifida are usually prone to constipation—either as a result of their lack of movement or as a side effect of medication. It is *very important* to make sure that constipation does not occur. Begin early—an infant of three months can already become constipated. Your doctor should be able to prescribe a supplement that can be added to formula or breast milk so as to guard against constipation. Keep your child on a diet high in fruit juices, fiber, and other stool-softening foods.

4) Because children with spina bifida usually don't walk, it's tempting to plunk them down in front of the TV while you go to the bathroom. You know there's no mischief they can get into, and you get your few moments of privacy. Don't give in to this temptation! Children with spina bifida need to observe others using the toilet if they are to learn to do so themselves.

CHILDREN WITH CEREBRAL PALSY

Many children with cerebral palsy (CP) can be toilet trained. When doing so, there are several factors to keep in mind:

1) Keep stools soft. Many children with cerebral palsy suffer from constipation. Sometimes this is a side effect of

medication; other times, it's due to inappropriate muscle tone. So keep your child's diet high in juices and fiber. If necessary, your doctor might prescribe a stool softener or laxative. (Don't administer any without your doctor's approval.)

2) Any potty chair or toilet seat adaptor must offer support for your child's body, and position her/him in such a way that abnormal muscle tone is minimized. Your child's feet *must* touch the floor. This will make it easier for her/him to push with her/his abdominal muscles. Toilet seat adaptors may need special equipment that will give your child adequate support.

3) Remember that your child's developmental age is more important than her/his chronological age. It may take longer for a child with CP to learn to use the potty.

4) Make sure your child's clothing is easy to handle. Zippers are easier than snaps or buttons, front openings are easier than back. Pants with elastic waistbands are the easiest of all. There are several special equipment suppliers that specialize in designing clothes for people with motor problems.

MENTALLY RETARDED CHILDREN

For generations, mentally retarded children were believed to be untrainable. Today we know that this is not the case. Most mentally retarded kids—even those who are profoundly retarded—*can* be trained, although it often takes them longer than it would take their non-retarded counterparts.

The method described below is equally effective for all retarded children, whether mildly, moderately, or profoundly retarded. Some will finish the process rather quickly—perhaps within a few months. Others may take longer—even up to a year or more. Of course, the more

sophisticated their level of functioning, and the older they
are, the less time it will take.

1) Make sure you're ready to embark upon the process,
attitudinally and in terms of your schedule.

2) Observe your child's excretory habits, perhaps keeping a little notebook on the subject.

3) Place your child on the potty at the anticipated times
of excretion. Additionally, set up a regular, predictable
schedule (say, every hour to hour and a half) for pottying
because you usually can't predict a urination schedule.

4) Be warm, loving, and nurturing.

5) Use the same terminology all the time. And be short
in your sentences. Rather than saying, "Okay, Jim, now
we're going to go to the potty," say "Potty time." You
want your child to focus on the critical word—potty—and
learn to associate it with the object (the potty), the activity
(urination or defecation), and the location (the bathroom).

6) Don't overdo the time spent on the potty—no more
than five to ten minutes and less if the child is squirmy.

7) Stay with your child.

8) Keep the potty in the bathroom. Moving the potty
about the house might be confusing. Allowing your child
to potty in the kitchen or den will not teach her/him about
privacy. Mentally retarded children often lack the conceptual apparatus enabling them to understand that when they
were little, they could make on a potty in the kitchen, but
suddenly the kitchen can no longer be used for that purpose.
From the beginning, they should be trained to do what
you'd like them to do for the rest of their lives.

9) Reward any production with smiles, hugs, and
kisses. Food treats are quite effective. One professional who
works with profoundly retarded children discovered that
colored candies (like M&M's) work best because they're
interesting to look at, as well as tasty. But raisins, peanuts,

potato chips, or whatever your child enjoys will work just fine.

10) When your child is using the potty regularly, begin dry pants checks. If the pants are dry, then say, "Dry!" and reward dryness with lots of praise and treats. If they are wet, say "Wet!" Don't judge your child, and don't express anger or disapproval. Simply say, "No wet," and provide dry pants. (If your child is verbal, you can use more sophisticated ways of communicating, such as, "Mom doesn't like wet pants" or, "Dad wants you to stay dry.") As your child gets older and more coordinated, have her/him become responsible for changing the wet clothes and depositing them in the laundry receptacle. If necessary, guide her/his hands.

11) The likelihood is that your child will begin to initiate toileting and signal her/his need to go. Some children, however—especially those who are profoundly retarded—may continue to need the schedule that you set up for them and for which you continue to assume responsibility.

12) Gradually withdraw the tangible rewards, reintroducing them only if your child regresses.

13) Some children learn nighttime dryness as well, though many remain in diapers at night for several years. Some never learn to remain dry at night. You might try the techniques suggested in Chapter 10, "Defining and Preventing Bed-wetting." Some mentally retarded children will respond quite nicely to them.

14) Once your child has mastered the basics of excreting in the potty, you can begin to teach some of the ancillary skills: pulling down the pants; sitting down on the chair without assistance; wiping her/his bottom; closing the lid; pulling up the pants again; flushing the toilet (once s/he's learned how to use the toilet); and washing and drying the hands. Don't overwhelm your child by trying to teach all these things at once. Instead concentrate on one new skill at a time.

Not all children will ultimately master all these skills. There may be a few who are profoundly retarded who may lack the coordination or the understanding of some of these steps.

CHILDREN WITH ATTENTION DEFICIT HYPERACTIVITY DISORDER (ADHD)

Hyperactive children are challenging, confounding, and wonderful (and often exhausting) all at the same time. Teaching them anything is quite a feat, because it's hard for them to attend to what you're presenting to them. Toilet training may present a problem for several reasons: The first is that they often suffer from developmental difficulties or subtle neurological irregularities that can affect motor control, cognitive ability, or communication (either receptive or expressive language). The second reason is that most of them won't have patience to sit on the potty for more than two minutes—if you're lucky.

1) Because most hyperactive children present so many practical challenges to their parents—not least of which is the sheer exhaustion of supervising them—they are often heartily resented. There's often an underlying feeling in parents that their child ''should'' be able to calm down and act just like everyone else. These feelings of resentment can lead to guilt on the parents' part, which, in turn, fosters more resentment. Every arena becomes a battleground in which the parent will prove that the child *can* learn to function just like all the other kids.

So begin with your attitude. If you can approach your child with inner peace, warmth, and love, half the battle is won.

2) Your child will have to exercise a great deal of control to remain seated for long enough to allow the bladder or rectal muscles to relax, the wastes to come out, and proper hygiene to be carried out. Make it worth her/his while! The more interesting and fun you make it, the more motivated your child will be to cooperate.

3) If your child is reluctant to sit on the potty, then experiment to see whether toys, books, or music might provide an additional incentive not to leave so quickly. If they distract her/him, however, and the process becomes dragged out because s/he's busy playing instead of making, you might want to leave the toys outside.

4) Rewards work very well with hyperactive children. Sugared snacks aren't a good idea, however, because some studies have linked consumption of sugars with hyperactivity.

5) There may be more daytime accidents than experienced by other children, as well as a higher incidence of bed-wetting.

6) If your child is on medication, then find out whether there are any side effects that may have an impact on toileting.

RESOURCES

• **Books.** Your library and bookstore are the best starting points. There are books available about special children in general and about each type of handicap in particular. Don't be surprised if some of the books either omit the subject of toilet training altogether or treat it superficially. But by reading several books, you might be able to glean a few useful points from each, and put together a program for yourself and your child.

In addition, here are some recommended books:

—California State Department of Education. *Learning Steps: A Handbook for Persons Working with Deaf-Blind Children in Residential Settings.*

—Cary, Jane Randolph. *How To Create Interiors for the Disabled: A Guidebook for Family and Friends.* New York: Pantheon books, 1978.

—Cunningham, Cliff, and Patricia Sloper *Helping Your Exceptional Baby: A Practical and Honest Approach to Raising a Mentally Handicapped Child.* New York: Pantheon books, 1978.

—Gorelick, Molly C., MD. *Toilet Training Your Retarded Child.*

—Kastein, Shulamith, Isabelle Spaulding, and Battia Scharf. *Raising the Young Blind Child: A Guide for Parents and Educators.* New York: Human Sciences Press, 1980.

—"The Joy of Special Parenting" in *Mothering* (Spring, 1987, pp. 91–96). Reprints are available by contacting *Mothering* at P.O. Box 1690, Santa Fe, NM 87504, (505) 984–8116 or FAX (505) 986–8335 (credit card orders only).

—Kaufman, Barry Neil. *Happiness Is a Choice.* New York: Random House, 1992.

—Kaufman, Barry Neil. *A Miracle to Believe In.* Garden City, New York: Doubleday and Co., 1982.

—Kaufman, Barry Neil. *Son-Rise.* New York: Warner Books, 1976.

—MacCracken, Mary. *A Circle of Children.* Philadelphia: Lippincott, 1974.

—McClurg, Eunice. *Your Down's Syndrome Child: Everything Today's Parents Need to Know About Raising Their Special Child.* Garden City, New York: Doubleday and Co., 1976.

—Pearl, Laura, and Kathleen Anton Scott. *Raising the Handicapped Child.* Englewood Cliffs: Prentice Hall, 1981.

—Stray-Gundersen, Karen, ed., *Babies with Down's Syndrome: A New Parents' Guide.* Maryland: Woodbine House, 1986.

—Sugar, Elayne C., and Casimir F. Firlit. "Urodynamic Biofeedback: A New Therapeutic Approach for Childhood Incontinence/Infection (vesical voluntary sphincter dyssynergia)": in *Journal of Urology,* vol. 128, December 1982, pp. 1253–1258.

—Valens, E. G. *The Other Side of the Mountain.* New York: Warner Books, 1978.

• There are national and local foundations set up to disseminate information dealing with most handicaps. They may or may not have toilet training information. Here are a few:

Option Institute and Fellowship, RD #1, Box 174A, Sheffield, MA 01257, (413) 229–2100.

Elayne Sugar or Ingrid Richards, Nurses and practitioners of Urodynamic biofeedback, Division of Urology, Children's Memorial Hospital, Northwestern University Medical School, Chicago, IL. 60607. (312) 880-4381 (Ingrid Richards) or (312) 880–4428 (Elayne Sugar).

American Deafness and Rehabilitation Association, P.O. Box 251554, Little Rock, AR 72225, (501) 663–7074.

Helen Keller Center for Deaf-blind Youths, 111 Middle Neck Road, Sands Point, NY 11050, (506) 944–8400 (ask for Daily Living Skills Department).

Attention Deficit Disorder Assoc., P.O. Box 2001, West Newberry, MA 01985, (303) 690–7548.

Association for Advancement of Blind and Retarded, 164–09 Hillside Avenue, Jamaica, NY 11432, (718) 523–2222.

Autism Society of America, 8601 Georgia Avenue, Suite 503, Silver Spring, MD 20910, (301) 565–0433.

Southern California Parent Support Group (Reversed Ostomies) 17406 Matinal Road, #5514 San Diego, CA 92127, (619) 673–7431 Attn: Ruth Rook.

National Autism Hot Line, Prichard Building, 605 Ninth Street, Huntington, WV 25710-0507, (304) 525–8014.

United Cerebral Palsy, 7 Penn Plaza (Suite 804), New York, NY 10001, (212) 268–6655. Look in the phone book for a local chapter. In case there isn't one in your area here's a national number: 1-800-872-5827.

American Association of the Deaf-Blind, 814 Thayer Avenue, Room 300, Silver Springs, MD 20910,

Spina Bifida Association of America, 4590 McArthur Boulevard, Suite 250, Washington DC 20007, 1-800-621-3141 (ask for Sue Libolt).

Association for Retarded Citizens, Look in the phone book for a local chapter which should be able to give you information, as well as put you in touch with other parents of retarded children. 900 Varnum Street NE, Washington, DC 20017, (202) 636–2950.

Parents of Children with Ostomies, United Ostomy Association, 36 Executive Park, Suite 120, Irvine, CA 92714-6744, 1-800-826-0826.

Kathleen Guardino, (718) 470–3637.
Ms. Guardino works with children whose temporary

ostomies were removed and must relearn how to recognize the need to urinate or defecate.

These are just a few of the national organizations set up to deal with children with special needs. There are, of course, local chapters, local hospital and community-center-sponsored support groups, and parent self-help groups. Schools for children with special needs are also excellent resources.

13

Stories

Here are some stories of parents who toilet trained their children, and how they went about it. These stories are fictional, but are inspired by real situations. They are designed to give you a flavor of what it's like to use the various approaches outlined in this book.

TOILET TRAINING FROM BIRTH

When Stacy was born, we were financially quite strapped. Every diaper saved was a few extra pennies in the bank. So I decided to start training her from birth. My husband thought this was strange at first, and he worried about it. He had been a psychology major in college and recalled learning that premature toilet training could be emotionally damaging.

We took a few long walks together and talked things over. It became real clear, after a while, that the important thing isn't the age when your kid is trained. The important thing is whether you're warm and loving. We decided that Freud and those other psychologists who warn against early toilet training were dealing with people who had been brought up with all that Victorian prudery and repression.

If we didn't act like prudes, or repress Stacy, she'd be just fine.

First I observed her very carefully for a few days. I really made it a focus. I didn't take phone calls or read a book while I nursed. I became really in tune with her body language. When she wrinkled her face and tightened her belly, I knew she was about to poop. She also would look sort of contemplative—like a little Buddha.

Next I bought a lap potty. Each time I nursed, I kept her diaper open on one side. As soon as I began to see those telltale signals, I arranged the potty under her little bottom. It felt like a major balancing act at first, but after some practice, I got it down pat. It was amazing how many movements I caught. It didn't happen each time, of course. Sometimes she'd go ahead and poop just after I'd closed her diaper up. But that was OK, too. I was catching a good many movements, and that was what counted. And I felt relaxed and comfortable, not like those Victorian parents whose kids ended up on Freud's couch.

I also developed the habit of checking her diaper regularly for dryness. If it was dry for more than an hour, I'd hold her on my lap over the potty and give her a water bottle to drink. Voilà! At least half the time, I'd be rewarded with this neat little stream, right into the potty. (Of course, once my hand slipped, and it landed on my skirt!)

As Stacy grew older, I began keeping a record of her bowel movements. There were weeks when she was very regular and predictable. I placed her on the lap potty when I expected her to make, and I usually wasn't disappointed. Of course, she wasn't always so neatly on schedule. There were many weeks when she didn't seem to be following any pattern at all. I noticed, though, that the more regulated our life-style was in terms of daily routine—like serving meals and putting her down for a nap at about the same time each day—the more regulated her movements were. I also kept track of her wetness and made a point of putting her on the potty when she had been dry for a while.

Soon I didn't need a lap potty anymore. Stacy was sitting by herself. I guess she was about six or seven months old when this happened. She was so proud of herself! She was only too glad to show off her new talent and sit on a regular potty. By this time, she had learned to connect the feeling of the potty around her bottom with peeing or pooping, and so most of the time, as soon as she felt the rim of the potty against her buttocks, whatever she had to produce would come right out.

Stacy was fully trained when she was about thirteen months old. By "trained" I don't mean that she told me when she needed to go. She was too busy scooting around the house, opening cabinets, and dumping out the contents of any accessible garbage cans. And certainly she was too little to take herself to the potty or even be left alone in the bathroom. She still had accidents. But she went willingly to the potty when I initiated it. And by eighteen months old, she was informing me by pointing to her genital area when she needed to go.

I definitely saved myself many diapers—at least half of what I would have otherwise used if I hadn't started training Stacy so early. It was fun for me to realize how much she could do and at such a young age! When my friends were struggling to get their two-year-olds interested in the potty, Stacy had been doing it for so long that it was no big deal. Like eating breakfast or getting dressed in the morning, pottying was part of her routine and no reason for fuss. Even though it took me more than a year to train her—and that's a long time—I enjoyed it.

TRAINING THE ONE-YEAR-OLD

My wife and I decided to train Brian early. Not really early, of course. But when he was maybe nine months old, we bought a potty and put it in the bathroom.

We talked to him a lot about the potty. We knew he didn't understand everything, but we figured that explaining things was a good habit to get into. We also took him into the bathroom with us from the beginning, instead of leaving him in the crib or playpen. So he was comfortable in the bathroom, and he had lots of opportunities to explore the potty.

He was really funny at first. He opened and closed the lid, stuck his toes inside, turned it upside down, and then tried to make the detachable bowl into a cup and drink from it. His antics were so adorable that my wife and I had many good laughs just watching him.

We bought some of those childrens' books about the potty. Brian loved to sit and turn the pages of books, especially when my wife and I were reading, too. We showed him the pictures and told him what the people in the book were doing.

One day, I sat him down on the potty. He looked sort of surprised, but when he saw that I was pleased, he smiled and stayed there for a few minutes. I noticed that he became restless, so I took him off and gave him a big hug. "Daddy's very proud!" I said.

We started to pay careful attention to his bowel schedule. Unfortunately, Brian was never one of these clockwork babies who produce in some predictable fashion. So we arbitrarily decided to put him on the potty every hour, for just a few minutes. And every time he sat, we hugged him and told him how proud we were.

Then one day it happened! I don't think Brian had the faintest idea at first just how that object landed in the bottom of the potty. But he was thrilled with my performance. I clapped and hugged him and twirled him around the room (which he loved). And the next time he sat and he urinated, I did the same thing. So did my wife. Well, I have a pretty smart kid. It didn't take him more than a few times to begin catching on. After several weeks, he began to have his movements and his urines more and more often in the potty. By about fourteen, maybe fifteen months, he was done!

Almost from the first time, my wife and I had been using the word "potty" to Brian whenever we took him. When he was fifteen months, he began saying "pot" each time he needed to use the potty. By two years old, he was signaling all the time, and we had almost completely stopped our reminders, unless we saw that he was super absorbed in something and was likely to ignore his need to use the bathroom.

It took longer to get him out of night diapers, though. He stayed wet at night until he was two and a half. But one morning, he was dry. Then the next morning. We put him in training pants, with a plastic shell over them during the night. By the time he was three, he didn't need the plastic shell anymore.

THE TWO-YEAR-OLD

I absolutely dreaded the day when Tommy would turn two. I'm a single mother, and the fabled terrible twos scared me out of my mind.

Sure enough, Tommy began throwing tantrums right on schedule. Actually, he had his first when he was nineteen months. He learned the word *no* and used it at me all the time. It drove me absolutely nuts. He became a difficult, obstinate child. I hate to say it, but I found myself calling him a brat in my own mind and dreading his company.

I couldn't imagine even trying to toilet train him. Tommy wouldn't sit still for two seconds. He lay down on the floor and kicked and screamed whenever I asked him to do something. I'd yell, and he'd scream even louder. How in the world would I ever get him to sit on the potty?

I was afraid to tell anyone about all this. The baby-sitter and I became like silent conspirators together as we pretended to the world that everything was OK with Tommy. I was so afraid someone would say that I couldn't make it as a single parent. I wasn't too clear about many things, but one thing I knew: I couldn't begin toilet training in such a depressed and confused state of mind. I just didn't know how to get out of it.

Then one day, a friend came over for lunch. Tommy was being so difficult, I couldn't hide what was happening from her. So I opened up and began talking to her. Turns out, one of her kids was also a pretty difficult kid at age two. I felt much better after sharing my feelings. She encouraged me to talk to a professional, so I made an appointment at our local counseling center.

Those sessions made such a difference! First of all, just being able to talk about everything helped. The counselor really listened to my concerns. She didn't try to tell me what to do or criticize me. There were many issues that came up, most of which didn't even have to do with Tommy at all! My relationship with my parents, my feelings after my divorce, even some issues going on between me and my boss at work. I went to the library and read some books about parenting. They also helped.

It took a few months, but at the end, I was ready to toilet train Tommy. I started by reading and watching videos with him. When I saw that he didn't have patience for books, I used Play-Doh, and we built dozens of little potties together. He loved watching me turn this glob of Play-Doh into a little boy who would sit on the potty. He loved even more squishing the "boy" between his fingers.

I didn't feel comfortable taking him into the bathroom with me. I know I would have felt differently if he had been a girl. I talked it over with my counselor, and she said that the main thing was my comfort—that there was no right or wrong in this. Well, at first I was sort of stumped. I felt it was important for him to see actual people use the bathroom, not just pictures in books. I finally asked Steven, the teenager next door, for help. Tommy absolutely adores and worships Steven. He follows him around, asks him to show him how to use a baseball bat or how to mow the lawn. Steven was glad to help out, and Tommy was fascinated.

By the time he was ready to try sitting on the potty himself, I felt a whole lot more relaxed—about everything, not just about the potty. He was getting lots of praise from me for doing what I wanted, and I wasn't yelling at him when he didn't listen to me. I carried over all these things into toilet training as well.

I was smiling and excited, and he picked up on my excitement. Nothing came out the first couple of times he sat, but I applauded him for sitting anyway, And when he made, I jumped up and down and clapped. I rewarded him with some raisins. He was pleased with himself and continued to repeat the performance. It went quickly and smoothly from there.

There was just one snag. When Tommy turned three, he started wetting himself again. At first I didn't think much of it. All kids go through occasional accidents. But it happened more and more. I saw the doctor, but there was nothing medically wrong. My therapist wondered if he was doing it for attention or needed more time with me. So I took a few days off from work and spent some extra time with him. The accidents seemed to slow up, but they were still happening.

One day I simply asked him, "Tommy, is there something bothering you?" And there was! I had been dating a man for a while, but it had recently taken a more serious turn. Tommy was jealous of the time I was spending with Brad. He had all sorts of fears about what would happen if

Brad and I got married. Once I reassured him of my love and straightened everything out with him, the accidents tapered off and eventually they stopped.

THE ONE-DAY APPROACH

My wife, Betty, and I both work. We have very demanding work schedules and are out of the house a good part of the time. Our daughter, Karen, is in the care of a wonderful baby-sitter. On the whole, we're very pleased with the arrangement. Just one thing—this baby-sitter positively and categorically refuses to have anything to do with toilet training. She doesn't mind diaper changing. But she has this idiosyncrasy—she won't touch potty training with a barge pole.

Betty and I were at a loss. We didn't know what we'd do. We couldn't take off from work for months and months while we brought Karen to the potty several times a day. Finally I happened on a book in the supermarket called *Toilet Training in Less Than a Day*. It seemed like a terrific idea, so I bought it. Betty and I read it cover to cover.

On the whole, we liked the idea very much. But there were a couple of things that just didn't sit right. So we decided to modify the program suggested by the authors. Here's what we did:

Although the authors said we could start as early as twenty months, we thought the whole thing would be more effective if we waited until Karen was completely verbal and completely out of the "twos." We were in no rush to get her out of diapers, and we figured that the older she was, the more cooperative she'd be.

My mother-in-law was having fits about our decision. *She* had trained all *her* children by the time they were a year old! (Of course, she never mentions that Betty's brother Jim wet his bed till he was twelve.) We reached a point where we were able to assert ourselves without getting angry, and explained to her that we weren't permissive or indifferent parents, and that Karen wouldn't grow up to be a wild hooligan with no social or moral values just because we waited until she was three to toilet train her. (Karen is eight now, and a well-behaved, delightful little girl.)

Once we had clarified our own thoughts and feelings, and ironed out our issues with my mother-in-law, we bought a bunch of children's books about the potty. At night, after dinner, these were the books we read to Karen. She loved them. Betty took her into the bathroom with her and explained what she was doing. We pointed out wet and dry things to her all the time, and whenever we noticed her making a Number One or a Number Two, we'd draw her attention to it.

We chose a weekend, and informed our friends and relatives that we were planning to toilet train Karen and didn't want to be disturbed except in an emergency. We informed Karen about a week ahead of time that we were planning to train her and asked her what she'd like to earn when she was done. She wanted a bike with training wheels! We told her that if she learned to use the potty, this meant that she was a big girl now and old enough to graduate from the tricycle to the training wheel bike. So she was very excited and eager to join in the training project.

Friday afternoon, Betty left work early and took Karen to the store to buy a potty and training pants. Karen loved the pants with little pink hearts and proudly displayed them to me when I came home.

Saturday morning, we removed Karen's diaper and said bye-bye to it. We put her in training pants for the first time.

We decided not to put the potty in the kitchen—we wanted her to know that the bathroom is the place for making, not the kitchen. We also decided not to make toilet training the all-consuming focus of the day. So we allowed her to watch TV, play games, go outdoors, and so on.

We did show her what to do on a wetting doll. Karen loves dolls, and she thought this was a lot of fun. We did conduct dry pants inspections and rewarded her with hugs, kisses, smiles, crackers, carrot sticks, and apple juice when she was dry. When she wet herself, we didn't scold her or disapprove in any way. We didn't make her practice correct toileting even once, let alone 10 times! We simply asked her to put her wet underwear in the laundry room and find herself a dry pair. At first she didn't want to. She was busy watching my wife plant tulip bulbs and didn't want to go into the house. But soon her underwear got cold, and she didn't like the feeling. She realized that wet panties feel very different from a wet diaper. She was only too glad to go into the house and get changed into dry clothes.

It worked well. By the end of Saturday, she was using the bathroom most of the time. She soiled her underwear once on Sunday morning, and we explained to her that the potty was for Number Twos as well. By Sunday evening she was almost completely trained.

The baby-sitter reported that she had only one accident on Monday. On Tuesday, she got through the day without a single accident! That afternoon, after work, we went and got her the tiniest, cutest little bike with training wheels. She was thrilled!

Karen slept in diapers for another few months. As she got older, we talked to her about nighttime dryness, and she learned to visit the toilet right before falling asleep. By the time she was about three and a half, she was out of diapers at night as well.

Oh, What a Relief It Is . . .

Congratulations! You've passed an important milestone in your child's life and development! With hope, it will be the first of many joyous journeys you'll undertake together with your child. May all the others be happy and successful as well.

If you can apply the lessons you've learned about toilet training—clarity of attitude, inner peace, love, acceptance, and respect for your child—to other situations in child-rearing as well, you will indeed be setting the stage for a wonderful parenting experience.

Good luck!